PROJECT BASED LEARNING

TOOLKIT SERIES

PBL FOR 21ST CENTURY SUCCESS

Teaching Critical Thinking, Collaboration, Communication, and Creativity

BUCK INSTITUTE
FOR EDUCATION

**PROJECT BASED LEARNING
FOR THE 21ST CENTURY**

Al Sommers

About the Buck Institute for Education

Founded in 1987, the Buck Institute for Education works to expand the effective use of Project Based Learning throughout the world. BIE is a mission-driven not-for-profit 501(c)3 organization based in Novato, California, and is a beneficiary of the Leonard and Beryl Buck Trust. BIE has provided PBL professional development services to thousands of educators, curriculum development consulting, and ongoing support for organizations including school districts, state departments of education, foundations, and other partners in the United States and around the world. BIE hosts annual *PBL World* conferences, and offers online resources at its website and online classes at **PBLU.org**. It publishes the *PBL Handbook*, which has sold over 40,000 copies, and the *PBL Toolkit Series* of books on how to do PBL. BIE publications have been translated into nine languages.

PBL FOR 21ST CENTURY SUCCESS

Principal Author: Suzie Boss
Editor: John Larmer
Contributing Editor: John R. Mergendoller, PhD

Published by Buck Institute for Education
18 Commercial Boulevard., Novato, California 94949 USA
bie.org

March 2013: First Edition.

Cover Photo by Anne Dowie, of students at Napa New Technology High School, California, with artifacts from a 3D printer project.

Printed by Unicorn Printing Specialists, San Rafael, California.
Printed on acid-free paper with soy-based ink.
Designed by Pam Scrutton, San Francisco, California.

ISBN 978-0-9740343-6-2

PROJECT BASED LEARNING
TOOLKIT SERIES

PBL FOR 21ST CENTURY SUCCESS

Table of Contents

TABLE OF CONTENTS

Foreword: About BIE's PBL Toolkit Series

The *PBL Toolkit Series* is designed to help teachers and schools do Project Based Learning more effectively. If PBL is not done right, or if it's done for the wrong reasons ("someone told us to do it"), it will be a waste of time. Incorporating PBL into your teaching is not like changing your textbook or incorporating a new Friday activity. PBL, done well, requires substantial changes in how teachers teach and how schools are organized.

PBL for 21st Century Success is the third in a series of short books on specific topics related to Project Based Learning. Each Toolkit is built around a combination of examples, guidance, and resources. The first book in the series is the *PBL Starter Kit*, which guides middle and high school teachers in planning and managing their first project. The second Toolkit is *PBL in the Elementary Grades*, for teachers in grades K-5. Other volumes in the series will be planned and published in response to the needs of the field.

More information and help can be found at the Buck Institute for Education's website, **bie.org**, including Project Search and Project Design tools, links to project libraries, and access to a PBL community of more than 20,000 educators where you can ask questions and contribute your ideas about various PBL topics. The website also provides excerpts from the acclaimed *PBL Handbook*, which has now been translated into nine languages, and allows you to order copies of this and other BIE publications. There are also summaries of PBL research, and information about BIE professional development and district and school coaching. Finally, don't miss the collection of videos of students and teachers planning and doing PBL, which you can access from the BIE website or through BIE's YouTube channel, **youtube.com/biepbl**.

All of us here at BIE wish you well, as you use PBL to help students develop the competencies they will need for 21st century success.

John R. Mergendoller, Ph.D.
Executive Director

Acknowledgments

Many people contributed ideas and inspiration for this book.

BIE Executive Director John Mergendoller and John Larmer, director of product development, recognized the need for this book and informed the contents with their valuable insights. Thanks to BIE staffers David Ross, Sara Hallermann, Alfred Solis, Lauren Scheller, Rosanna Mucetti, and Jason Ravitz for sharing their expertise and constructive feedback.

BIE National Faculty members contributed in significant ways. Special thanks to Jill Ackers, Charity Allen, Rody Boonchouy, and Tim Kubik.

Many teachers and school leaders provided noteworthy project examples and supporting materials to demonstrate 21st century learning in action. Thanks for the valuable contributions from Nicole Lentino, Tammy Parks, Amy Carrington, Leah Penniman, Maria Alzugaray, Abby Benedetto, and Shelley Wright. Bob Lenz of Envision Education and Paul Curtis from the New Tech Network shared their insights about the hard work of school change to meet the needs of today's learners and better prepare them for 21st century success. Thanks also to the Metropolitan Nashville School District for their thoughtful critique of our rubrics.

INTRODUCTION

A growing urgency to prepare students for 21st century challenges has many educators looking for new instructional approaches. Mastery of academic content remains important, but it's no longer enough. Students also need to develop the "process skills" that will help them navigate their rapidly changing world.

To meet these new demands, more and more teachers are turning to Project Based Learning, or PBL. PBL puts equal emphasis on academic learning goals and on the competencies students need more than ever in the 21st century. Through well-designed project experiences, students learn how to contribute to team efforts, think critically, solve problems creatively, and communicate effectively, all while engaging in deep learning of important content.

We know that the shift to PBL creates new questions for teachers: How do I design projects to meet goals for both content mastery and 21st century learning? What does 21st century learning mean, anyway? Is it fair to assess students on hard-to-measure skills like creativity? How can I find time to focus on goals like learning to collaborate when I'm scrambling to meet the new Common Core State Standards?

This book offers practical answers to help you and your students get a better handle on 21st century competencies.

The Purpose of This Book

The benefits of PBL are compelling, but they aren't automatic. After years of experience with this instructional approach, we know that students need to be supported by teachers who understand how to design, manage, and assess high-quality PBL. Other books in the Buck Institute for Education Toolkit Series, as well as our intensive professional development programs, focus in depth on PBL processes that lead to high-quality learning experiences. (Learn more about the PBL Toolkit Series and professional development opportunities at our website, **bie.org**)

This book will help you expand your PBL toolkit with practical strategies for teaching specific 21st century competencies to middle school and high school students. We also offer guidance

> The 4 C's—critical thinking, collaboration, creativity, and communication—are a natural fit with PBL.

on how to assess these competencies. Although there are many competing definitions of 21st century learning, we focus here on the four competencies that we consider most essential. These 4 C's — critical thinking, collaboration, creativity, and communication — are a natural fit with PBL.

One additional note: In this book we have chosen to move beyond the commonly used term "21st century skills" in favor of "21st century competencies." We think it's more accurate to describe someone as "competent" in, say, thinking critically, rather than saying he or she has the "skill" to do so. The 4 C's are complex sets of competencies, which often involve more than a single skill. If students are competent communicators, they are able to organize information, time its delivery, read the audience reaction, and change the message they had intended to give right there on the spot. As our rubrics suggest, good communicators need to be competent in a variety of areas; they don't simply exercise a single communication skill.

How to Use This Book

This book is designed to help you deliberately teach and assess the 4 C's in the context of well-designed projects. You will gain a better picture of what this looks like from the detailed project close-ups you will find in each chapter. Then, to help you teach and assess each of the 4 C's in your own projects, we take you though a three-part approach. We call it Design-Develop-Determine. In each of the upcoming chapters, we will walk you through how you can use the "3 D's" to help you and your students master the "4 C's." At each stage of Design-Develop-Determine, you'll be prompted to consider key questions. For example:

- **Design**: When you are designing a project, how can you find opportunities to focus on specific 21st century competencies? Which types of projects, Driving Questions, and products work best for developing specific competencies?

- **Develop:** When students are engaged in the project, how are you developing their understanding of what each of the 4 C's means, and their ability to apply them? How can you incorporate learning activities that will support and strengthen their development of these competencies?

- **Determine**: At the end of the project, how can you determine, through your assessment strategies, that students have become more proficient at applying the 4 C's? How can you help them reflect on what they've gained?

How you use the book will depend on your prior experiences with PBL and your professional learning goals. For example:

- **If you are new to PBL,** use this book to build your understanding of the project approach. You may want to read this book in tandem with the *PBL Starter Kit*, which provides a more detailed introduction for middle and high school teachers to all phases of project planning, management, and assessment. (BIE's PBL Toolkit Series book for K-5 teachers is *PBL in the Elementary Grades*.)

- **If you have a basic understanding of PBL** — perhaps you've tried a project or two — use this book to sharpen your focus on students' 21st century competencies and troubleshoot challenges. You may, for example, want to know more about how to explicitly *teach* and *assess* specific competencies, rather than simply assume students are learning them in a project.

- **If you are a PBL veteran**, use this book to go even deeper with 21st century learning goals. For example, you may be ready to tackle projects that take students into the community, address global learning goals, or use technology to connect with other classrooms for deeper inquiry.

- **If you are an instructional coach or school leader**, use this book to frame conversations with teachers and inform classroom observations of 21st century PBL in action. You may find the book helpful for sharing with parents and other community members who are interested in preparing students for college and careers. The last chapter contains guidance for building support for 21st century learning among parents and your community, as well as advice for creating system-wide policies and practices that will support teachers as they implement PBL.

You can also use this book to integrate technology into PBL. Instead of treating technological know-how as a separate 21st century competency, we have incorporated suggestions for technology use to address each of the 4 C's.

This book also contains guidance on meeting the needs of English learners in a PBL environment. Look for tips scattered throughout plus several special notes in the Communication chapter.

> We have incorporated suggestions for technology use to address each of the 4 C's.

Special Features Ahead

Throughout the book, watch for these special features and call-outs:

 What Should You See?

Where should you focus your attention during a visit to a PBL classroom if you want to find evidence of 21st century learning?

In each of the upcoming chapters, we offer a list of questions to keep in mind if you want to know whether students are developing their capacity as critical thinkers, collaborators, communicators, or creative thinkers. If you are an administrator doing classroom walk-throughs, instructional coach, or curious parent — or a teacher seeking to improve your own PBL practice — you can use these questions to guide your observations and reflections.

Remember, one of the best ways to understand what's happening in a busy PBL classroom is to ask students. They should be able to explain what they're working on and which strategies are helping them make progress toward answering their Driving Question.

TIP FROM THE **CLASSROOM** is a signal to listen for ideas you can borrow from experienced PBL teachers.

Bulletin Board Here you'll find examples, resources, and closer looks at strategies you can use to support students.

TECH TIP A wide range of technology tools can be integrated into PBL to expand and deepen opportunities for authentic, rigorous learning. Each of the upcoming chapters suggests tech tools to help with specific 21st century competencies.

For starters, here's a tip to support your exploration of 21st century learning through PBL:

TECH TIP Join the Conversation

Become part of an international conversation about PBL by joining the PBL Community on Edmodo, a free social network dedicated to education (**edmodo. com/biepbl**). You will find an active online community for exchanging ideas and resources with teaching colleagues, along with an ever-expanding set of PBL tools, videos, and other materials from BIE. It's a great platform for asking questions, inviting feedback, and reflecting on your own professional growth as a PBL teacher. If Edmodo is new to you, don't let that stop you. There's no better way to model being a 21st century learner than to learn something new yourself!

What's Essential in PBL

Before we go further with our exploration of 21st century competencies, let's be sure we're starting on the same page when it comes to talking about Project Based Learning.

What do we mean by PBL? We know from experience that good projects can vary widely. They might last only a week or two, or continue for an entire term. They can focus on one subject area or take an interdisciplinary approach. Regardless of the differences, well-designed PBL shares common elements.

Here's how we define this approach:

> *Project Based Learning is a systematic teaching method that engages students in learning important knowledge and developing 21st century competencies through an extended, student-influenced inquiry process structured around complex, authentic questions and carefully designed products and learning tasks.*

When PBL is working according to plan, you should see a high degree of student engagement. Rather than asking, "Why do I need to learn this?", students are driven by their own inquiry. We often say that a project gives students a strong Need to Know. What's more, students are able to apply what they are learning to solve an authentic problem or address an issue that they care about. They know how to communicate their findings to a public audience. It adds up to meaningful and lasting learning.

Whatever form a project takes, it must have these eight essential elements to meet our definition of high-quality PBL:

Significant Content: At its core, the project is focused on teaching students important knowledge and skills, derived from standards and key concepts at the heart of academic subject areas.

21st Century Competencies: Students build competencies valuable for today's world, such as critical thinking/problem solving, collaboration, communication, and creativity/innovation, which are taught and assessed.

In-Depth Inquiry: Students are engaged in a rigorous, extended process of asking questions, using resources, and developing answers.

Driving Question: Project work is focused by an open-ended question that students explore or that captures the task they are completing.

> When PBL is working according to plan, you should see a high degree of student engagement.

Need to Know: Students see the need to gain knowledge, understand concepts, and apply skills in order to answer the Driving Question and create project products, beginning with an Entry Event that generates interest and curiosity.

Voice and Choice: Students are allowed to make some choices about the products to be created, how they work, and how they use their time, guided by the teacher and depending on age level and PBL experience.

Revision and Reflection: The project includes processes for students to use feedback to consider additions and changes that lead to high-quality products, and think about what and how they are learning.

Public Audience: Students present their work to other people, beyond their classmates and teacher.

Watch for mention of these eight elements throughout the book.

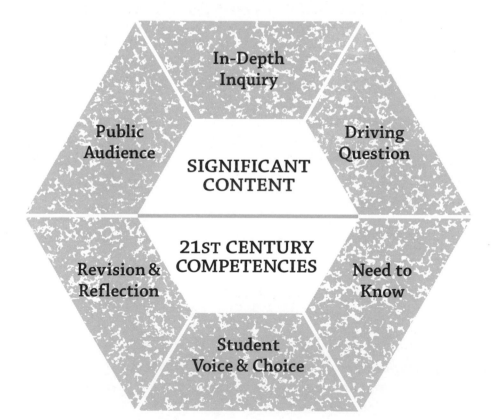

COMPETENCIES FOR COLLEGE, CAREERS, AND LIFE

The 21st century learning movement may be in its second decade, but that doesn't mean traditional instruction has gone the way of the chalkboard. In many classrooms, learning still involves memorization of superficial facts rather than deep exploration of rich content. Students who spend the bulk of their time on content coverage miss opportunities to apply what they are learning. As a result, they may not fully develop the problem-solving and thinking strategies they will need for the future. This book is intended to accelerate the shift by showing you how to use Project Based Learning to deliver 21st century results.

Well designed projects enable students to master important academic content while also teaching them — through firsthand experience — how to solve problems, collaborate, think critically, and communicate effectively. Good projects help students learn about the larger world, too, engaging them with issues and experts in their own communities as well as around the globe. Students practice thinking critically as they evaluate sources, question experts, and deepen their information literacy skills. They think creatively when they generate innovative solutions and improve on each other's ideas. They become proficient communicators when they leverage technology to reach their intended audience. Such rich learning experiences prepare students for active citizenship, both online and in "real life."

This mash-up of content and competencies helps students prepare to tackle the complex challenges ahead of them. A well-prepared college freshman, for instance, should be able to conduct research, make coherent arguments, collaborate with a peer group on an extended out-of-class project, and manage time effectively (Conley, 2011). That's because learning at the college level is changing, too, demanding more from students than simply summing up what they've heard in a lecture hall.

Looking beyond college or other post-secondary training, we know that many students will be heading into career fields not yet imagined, using technology tools not yet invented, and solving problems we can't predict. Even those who enter more familiar career fields will need to be ready for rapid change. In schools that encourage PBL, students are getting a head start on the unpredictable future by learning what it means to work well with diverse colleagues, and be flexible and nimble enough to respond to changing circumstances.

> PBL builds readiness for college, career, and the responsibilities of citizenship.

Research on PBL and 21st Century Readiness

From our work with hundreds of K-12 schools, we have seen how PBL builds readiness for college, career, and the responsibilities of citizenship. When PBL is implemented with attention to the essential elements for project success (summarized in the Introduction), this instructional approach proves to be effective for teaching both academic content and the "process skills" involved in problem solving.

Research reinforces what practitioners tell us about PBL:

- Teachers who had the benefit of long-term professional development to help them become proficient in all phases of PBL were more likely to both teach and assess 21st century competencies. Although their students spent more time on learning activities that involved problem solving, collaboration, idea generation, and public speaking, they scored at least as well on standardized tests as students learning content through more traditional, lecture-and-test-based instruction (Hixson, Ravitz, & Whisman, 2012).

- In high school economics classes, a large-scale study in California and Arizona showed that students taught with project-based units not only learned more economics content than peers in non-PBL classes, but they also learned to be better problem solvers (Finkelstein, Hanson, Huang, Hirschman, & Huang, 2009; Mergendoller, Maxwell, & Bellisimo, 2007).

- Schools implementing a PBL model in urban settings showed substantial progress in closing the achievement gap for students eligible for free or reduced-price lunch, English learners, and African-American and Hispanic students (Expeditionary Learning, 2011).

- Urban middle school students in Detroit who were taught with a project-based approach scored better on state tests of both science content knowledge and science process skills than students who had been taught traditionally (Clay-Chambers, 2008).

- Middle school and high school teachers using open-ended problem solving and other reform-oriented mathematics curricula achieved a reduction in linguistic, ethnic, and class inequalities in their schools. Compared with students taking a procedural, skills-based approach to learning math, those taking an open-ended approach attained not only a higher level of achievement but also more equal achievement (Boaler, 2002).

*For more information about the extensive research supporting PBL, visit the BIE online library (**bie.org**) or see the research summary in **Useful Stuff**.*

PBL and School Change

It's no wonder that PBL is gaining traction as one of the best methods to prepare students for a fast-changing, complex world. To help students get ready for the future, many networks of schools, districts, and even entire states are adopting Project Based Learning as a primary method of instruction. As you will see in the examples ahead, PBL gives students opportunities to practice and get better at ways of learning and working that will serve them well in college, in careers, and in life. Experience and research also tell us that, the more comfortable teachers are with PBL, the more time their students will spend on problem solving, teamwork, creative challenges, and other learning activities that develop 21st century competencies.

Widespread adoption of the Common Core State Standards is likely to further accelerate the shift to PBL. The new standards put a premium on interdisciplinary thinking, especially when it comes to integrating the English language arts. PBL naturally leads to learning across disciplines as students investigate real-world questions that don't fit neatly into content silos. Critical thinking, also strongly emphasized throughout the CCSS, is strengthened in inquiry-driven projects that motivate students to ask hard questions, dig deep for understanding, and defend their arguments with reliable evidence. In math, the standards call for the authentic problem solving that is a hallmark of high-quality projects. (See pages 13-16 for a closer look at how PBL addresses the Common Core.)

> PBL naturally leads to learning across disciplines as students investigate real-world questions that don't fit neatly into content silos.

A Growing Urgency

Why are educators feeling such urgency when it comes to preparing students for the challenges ahead? Consider these trends:

- According to analysis by the International Youth Foundation (2012), "The capacity to think critically, solve problems, communicate effectively, and work in teams are some of the life skills highly valued by employers, but these skills are not addressed effectively in most formal educational curricula."

- In a survey of CEOs, corporate leaders named creativity as the quality they most value in employees (IBM, 2010). However, creativity scores measured by the Torrance Test of Creative Thinking have been in decline since the 1990s, with the drop most precipitous for students in grades K-6 (Bronson & Merryman, 2010).

- Employers report a shortage of candidates who know how to work in teams, think creatively, and interact effectively with colleagues or potential customers. This disconnect between what employers want and what youth bring to the table has major economic consequences (Aspen Institute, 2008).

- To respond to the call for a new generation of innovators, several states are in the early stages of developing indexes that will compare what schools are doing to build students' creative and critical thinking potential (Robelen, 2012).

A Tale of Two High Schools

To appreciate how acquisition of 21st century competencies might improve this picture, let's hear from a mother whose two sons had dramatically different high school experiences:

"Our oldest son attended the same comprehensive high school that his father had attended. Nothing had changed since his dad was a student there," she said. Her husband even recognized the same test on *Romeo and Juliet* that he had taken a generation earlier. Although their son earned good grades at his traditional high school, he later struggled in college classes that challenged him to think on his feet, manage his time, and collaborate with team members.

When it was time for her youngest son to start high school, it was a different story. Just in time for his freshman year, the local school was redesigned to emphasize Project Based Learning, integrate technology across the curriculum, and make other changes to better meet the needs of 21st century learners. Their son thrived in this challenging environment, which left him well-prepared for life after high school.

"The contrast is incredible," she said. "Our youngest son approaches his education so differently. Now that he's a college student, the first thing he does in a new class is organize a study group so that he has a team of peers to collaborate with. If he has questions, he doesn't hesitate to follow up with his professors or seek information on his own. Unlike his older brother, he really owns his education."

PBL makes school more meaningful and engaging *right now*.

Although the 21st century learning movement has tended to focus on preparing students for college and careers, there's a more immediate reason why PBL is gaining traction. It makes school more meaningful and engaging *right now*. Not surprisingly, student engagement and motivation to learn increase when students take part in PBL. That's especially true when students see projects as relevant and connected to their lives. (See *PBL Research Summary* in **Useful Stuff** for more information.)

By designing projects that emphasize essential 21st century competencies along with academic content, we can prepare more students to become engaged, self-directed learners, interested in the learning at hand and better prepared for the challenges ahead.

The 4 C's, and Then Some

Educational researchers, policymakers, corporate leaders, and others from diverse sectors have invested considerable energy in defining what today's students need to know and be able to do by the time they complete their K-12 education.

> It's not authentic PBL unless students are working together, thinking critically and creatively to solve problems, and sharing what they know with a public audience.

Frameworks such as the National Educational Technology Standards for Students, for example, focus on what students should be able to accomplish by using technology to communicate, connect, and create. The Big6 Skills (**big6.com**) emphasize thinking critically about the sources and reliability of information. Many experts emphasize global awareness and cultural competency as the keys to thriving in our flattened, hyper-connected world. Other well-reasoned calls-to-action focus on the need for increased character education and media literacy among today's young people. At the same time, we all recognize the need to help students grow into their role as active, engaged citizens.

This may seem like an impossibly long list of learning goals. The Partnership for 21st Century Skills sums up the most essential capabilities as the "4 C's": critical thinking, collaboration, communication, and creativity. These naturally come into play during projects. In fact, it's not authentic PBL unless students are working together, thinking critically and creatively to solve problems, and sharing what they know with a public audience.

In the coming chapters, we'll take a closer look at how to deliberately teach and assess each of the 4 C's through PBL. For now, here's a preview of what students gain when they have opportunities to develop these capabilities:

- **Critical Thinking**: Students are able to analyze, evaluate, and understand complex systems; investigate questions for which there are no clear-cut answers; evaluate different points of view or sources of information; draw appropriate conclusions based on evidence and reasoning; and apply strategies to solve problems.

- **Collaboration**: Students work effectively and respectfully with diverse groups to solve problems and accomplish a common goal. They assume shared responsibility for completing tasks. Team efforts are "greater than the sum of their parts"; student teams accomplish better results than could be done by individuals working alone.

- **Communication**: Students communicate effectively both face-to-face and across multiple media and for various purposes. They are able to organize their thoughts, data, and findings, and share these effectively through a variety of media. They communicate well both orally and in writing. Technology fluency enables them to select and use the right medium for their message.

- **Creativity and Innovation**: Students generate and improve on original ideas and also work creatively with others. They are able to generate and refine solutions to complex problems or tasks based on synthesis, analysis, and then combine or present what they have learned in new and original ways.

Discussions of what students need to know and be able to do for 21st century readiness include a long list of additional habits of mind and capabilities. Some experts argue that the best thing educators can do for students is to help them discover their passions. Having the mindset to persist despite setbacks is also critical, of course, along with self-management skills such as knowing how to set goals and manage time and resources.

These are all important goals, and projects may, indeed, help students develop many of these abilities and habits of mind. Rather than taking a scattershot approach to try to cover them all, we have chosen to focus in depth on the 4 C's. If you help students build a strong foundation in these four competencies, along with a deep understanding of academic content, they should be well prepared for 21st century success.

> Students need opportunities to grow into the new set of competencies that comes with the territory in PBL.

A Developmental Approach

Just as teachers need time (and sometimes coaching) to become skillful facilitators of Project Based Learning, so do students need opportunities to grow into the new set of competencies that comes with the territory in PBL. Students who arrive at middle school or high school with no prior experience in PBL will likely need to start with the basics when it comes to working with team members, speaking in public, or generating original ideas.

That's why we take a developmental approach when describing classroom strategies that build 21st century competencies. Rely on your assessment of students' current abilities, including their English language proficiency. Take their prior experiences into consideration as you determine how much support students will need as they move along the continuum from novice to expert. As students become more capable of driving their own learning, you can gradually remove the training wheels.

PBL and Common Core — and Next Generation Science Standards

With the Common Core State Standards adopted by all but a handful of states, efforts are underway across the country to help students meet the higher bar that the new standards set. The overarching goal of the new standards is to better prepare students for college and careers. PBL, with its emphasis on both significant content and 21st century competencies, addresses these new standards in several important ways.

> As states move toward implementation of the Common Core, more and more schools and districts are focusing on PBL.

David Ross, director of professional development for BIE, offers this pithy analysis about the alignment of PBL and the Common Core:

> *Everyone knows that content is king and Common Core wears the crown. Significant content is one of our eight Essential Elements of PBL. Make an easy connection: Significant Content = Common Core. Now let's use a shorter word. When designing a rigorous, relevant, and engaging project, Common Core is the "what." But what about the "how?" In our minds the answer is obvious: PBL is the solution for Common Core implementation. PBL is the "how."*

Of course, we realize that PBL is not the only way to help students master these new standards. As states move toward implementation of the Common Core, however, more and more schools and districts are focusing on PBL as their go-to instructional strategy to prepare students for deeper thinking. Next-generation assessments aligned to the new standards (still in development at this writing) are expected to emphasize application of knowledge rather than recall of facts. Here, too, we find common ground with PBL, in which students demonstrate and share what they know or can do through performance assessments. For PBL veterans, student demonstrations of learning are not new at all. They're an essential element of every project.

Content-area experts have reached similar conclusions. The National Council of Teachers of English, for example, emphasizes that teachers determine the "how" when it comes to addressing the call for increased rigor and an emphasis on nonfiction reading in the new standards:

> *Teachers who immerse their students in rich textual environments, require increasing amounts of reading, and help students choose ever more challenging texts will address rigor as it is defined by the CCSS. This means keeping students at the center, motivating them to continually develop as writers and readers,*

and engaging them in literacy projects that are relevant to their lives. (Wessling, Lillge, & VanKooten, 2011, p. 11).

Common Core Standards for English Language Arts include tasks that are very familiar to people who know PBL:

- *Conduct short as well as more sustained research projects based on focused questions*

- *Prepare for and participate effectively in a range of conversations and collaborations with diverse partners*

- *Use technology, including the Internet, to produce and publish writing and to interact and collaborate with others*

- *Conduct short research projects to answer a question (including a self-generated question)*

These new ELA standards go beyond reading and writing, effectively laying out "a vision of what it means to be a literate person in the twenty-first century. Indeed, the skills and understandings students are expected to demonstrate have wide applicability outside the classroom or workplace." This emphasis on real-world learning is nothing new to PBL teachers who routinely connect projects with the world beyond the classroom.

Common Core Standards of Mathematical Practice also echo PBL best practices.

Common Core Standards of Mathematical Practice also echo PBL best practices. The math standards set expectations for students to do real-world problem solving, use mathematical modeling, apply statistical analysis, and communicate their understanding. "Mathematically proficient students can apply the mathematics they know to solve problems arising in everyday life, society, and the workplace," according to the *Standards of Mathematical Practice*. Such applications naturally have a place within high-quality projects that ask students to use mathematics concepts and procedures in authentic contexts.

Read Closely, Think Critically, Communicate Purposefully

You shouldn't have to reinvent the wheel to ensure that your students meet the Common Core. Rather, by focusing on best practices for designing, managing, and assessing high-quality projects, you and your students will be on your way to meeting the new standards. The Common Core standards build skills in a gradual, age-appropriate pace over the grade levels. So, too, should you take a developmental approach to building your students' competencies and understanding through PBL.

Recurring themes in the Common Core are worth considering as you plan projects:

Emphasize inquiry: In-depth inquiry is an Essential Element of PBL and a goal of the Common Core. The standards emphasize both short, tightly focused research projects (similar to what often happens in the world of work) and longer, in-depth investigations that require collaborative efforts.

Emphasis on nonfiction texts: By high school, students are expected to focus 70 percent of their reading on nonfiction texts. Students will need to read carefully for understanding and think critically about content as they engage with a variety of nonfiction texts. As literacy experts point out in *Pathways to the Common Core*, the standards "call for students to move away from simply reading for information, toward reading with a more analytical stance" (Calkins, Ehrenworth, & Lehman, 2012, p. 20). PBL provides a motivating context for critical nonfiction reading. In inquiry-based projects, students read with a purpose to answer their own questions. Reading and writing across the curriculum, as the Common Core calls for, goes hand-in-hand with interdisciplinary PBL.

Emphasis on critical thinking: Common Core calls on students to make arguments that are supported by evidence; in other words, to be critical thinkers. Developing a defensible argument may involve conducting research or surveys, making observations, or evaluating sources for reliability or bias. (Chapter 2 takes a closer look at strategies to encourage critical thinking within PBL.)

Emphasis on problem solving: Authentic problem solving is emphasized in the Common Core. The high school standards call on students to practice applying mathematical ways of thinking to real-world issues and challenges. The goal is not memorization, but rather the ability to think and reason mathematically so that students will be able to apply their understanding of math to novel concepts. That aligns with the practical application of knowledge that happens in PBL.

Emphasis on communication: Being able to present knowledge and ideas effectively, with the appropriate use of technology, is another Common Core goal that aligns with PBL practices. At the end of a project, students typically present their work to an authentic audience. By the time students are in high school, they should be able to tailor their presentations to appeal to specific audiences. Student interactions with experts and other adults from outside the classroom create a context in which they will need to use formal English and also use discipline-specific vocabulary to discuss project details.

In the next four chapters, as we take a closer look at each of the key 21st century competencies, watch for the graphic illustrations that call out opportunities to

> In-depth inquiry is an Essential Element of PBL and a goal of the Common Core.

address Common Core State Standards across the span of a project. In **Useful Stuff**, find rubrics for assessing each of the 4 C's that are aligned to the Common Core.

Next Generation Science Standards

The new national standards proposed for K-12 science shift the focus of instruction from simply acquiring content knowledge to the practice of science skills. Many of the draft Next Generation Science Standards align with practices common to 21st century Project Based Learning. For example, look at what students are supposed to learn how to do in the "Science and Engineering Practices" section:

1. Asking questions (for science) and defining problems (for engineering)

2. Developing and using models

3. Planning and carrying out investigations

4. Analyzing and interpreting data

5. Using mathematics and computational thinking

6. Constructing explanations (for science) and designing solutions (for engineering)

7. Engaging in argument from evidence

8. Obtaining, evaluating, and communicating information

Some of the standards could actually be used as a stand-alone project idea, such as, "Design, evaluate, and refine a solution for reducing negative impact of human activities on the environment and ways to sustain biodiversity and maintain the planet's natural capital" (HS-LS2-j). Even when the standards do not have an explicit project-based tone, there is a focus on the key competencies needed for PBL: inquiry, communication, and critical thinking. Consider what students are asked to demonstrate in order to meet the "College and Career Readiness" standards: "applying a blend of science and engineering practices... approach problems not previously encountered by the student" and "self-directed planning, monitoring, and evaluation." Sounds like what happens in PBL!

> Science standards for College and Career Readiness sound like what happens in PBL!

CRITICAL THINKING IN PBL

Discussions of 21st century learning consistently emphasize the need for critical thinking, as if this were a new goal for education. Of course, these competencies are far from new. The teachings of Socrates — exhorting us to seek evidence and examine assumptions for bias or faulty logic — are as applicable today as they were 2,500 years ago.

Although critical thinking has been with us for centuries, the need for better critical thinkers has grown more urgent in the Information Age. Making an informed decision is more challenging when there is so much information to search and evaluate for reliability. Meanwhile, automation is changing the nature of modern workplaces. With many of yesterday's jobs becoming obsolete, those who can demonstrate complex thinking are in high demand. Employers asked to predict which attributes would be most valuable in the near future put critical thinking at the top of their list (Conference Board, 2006).

Not surprisingly, being able to think critically is now considered a key to college readiness. Students who excel at memorization in high school arrive at college unprepared to engage in a give-and-take of ideas, evaluate evidence, reach conclusions, or make convincing arguments. "The college instructor is more likely to emphasize a series of key thinking skills that students, for the most part, do not develop extensively in high school," reports *Redefining College Readiness* (Conley, 2007). Looking beyond college and careers, we can see the need for critical thinkers to help society address an array of complex problems with global implications. Tackling challenges involving public health, poverty, energy, or economics — sometimes called "wicked problems" or "grand challenges" because of their complexity and scale — demands skillful thinkers who can understand how systems work and anticipate the consequences and implications of potential solutions. On a smaller scale, local issues often require the same kind of careful analysis from community members. From the polling place to the workplace, all of us need to be able to evaluate information and approach both problems and solutions with a critical lens.

Critical Thinking and the Common Core

The Common Core State Standards set high expectations for students to become skilled critical thinkers as they progress from K-12. Read the standards closely and you will find repeated use of these words and phrases: analyze, read closely, make logical inferences, cite sources, interpret, integrate, evaluate, make decisions. In specific ways, these describe the actions of a critical thinker.

Anchor Standards for Reading:

▶ Read closely to determine what the text says explicitly and to make logical inferences from it; cite specific textual evidence when writing or speaking to support conclusions drawn from the text.

▶ Analyze the structure of texts, including how specific sentences, paragraphs, and larger portions of the text (e.g., a section, chapter, scene, or stanza) relate to each other and the whole.

▶ Assess how point of view or purpose shapes the content and style of a text.

▶ Integrate and evaluate content presented in diverse media and formats, including visually and quantitatively, as well as in words.

▶ Delineate and evaluate the argument and specific claims in a text, including the validity of the reasoning as well as the relevance and sufficiency of the evidence.

▶ Analyze how two or more texts address similar themes or topics in order to build knowledge or to compare the approaches the authors take.

Anchor Standards for Writing:

▶ Produce clear and coherent writing in which the development, organization, and style are appropriate to task, purpose, and audience.

▶ Conduct short as well as more sustained research projects based on focused questions, demonstrating understanding of the subject under investigation.

▶ Gather relevant information from multiple print and digital sources, assess the credibility and accuracy of each source, and integrate the information while avoiding plagiarism.

▶ Draw evidence from literary or informational texts to support analysis, reflection, and research.

Anchor Standards for Speaking and Listening:

▶ Evaluate a speaker's point of view, reasoning, and use of evidence and rhetoric.

▶ Present information, findings, and supporting evidence such that listeners can follow the line of reasoning and the organization, development, and style are appropriate to task, purpose, and audience.

Standards for Mathematical Practice:

▶ Make sense of problems and persevere in solving them. ("analyze givens, constraints, relationships, and goals")

▶ Construct viable arguments and critique the reasoning of others. ("justify their conclusions, communicate them to others, and respond to the arguments of others")

▶ Model with mathematics. ("apply mathematics to solve problems arising in everyday life, society, and the workplace")

In **Useful Stuff** you can find a rubric assessing critical thinking that is aligned to the Common Core.

Thinking Across the Curriculum

Over the years, many fine minds have wrestled with defining critical thinking. Part of the challenge comes from the requirements of different disciplines. The nature of evidence may be different in science or math than in social studies or English, for example. Yet despite sometimes subtle distinctions, there is a connecting thread of teaching students to make well-reasoned, thoughtful judgments in every field.

Roland Case of The Critical Thinking Consortium suggests that we do students a disservice if we too narrowly define discrete thinking skills and processes. Students faced with a laundry list of thinking skills — research, problem solving, decision making, goal setting, predicting, comparing, and so forth — may lose sight of the big picture of why critical thinking matters. "As long as critical thinking remains but one type among many forms of thinking, there will never be adequate time devoted to it" (Case, 2005, p. 45). Case also raises the concern that, if critical thinking is categorized as higher-order thinking, then it may mistakenly be reserved for only top-achieving students. Lower achievers may get stuck in lower-order thinking, lacking opportunities to hone their critical faculties. Likewise, Case cautions against separating thinking skills from content mastery in the classroom. "Thinking without content is vacuous, and content acquired without thought is mindless and inert" (Case, p. 47). Instead, Case recommends embedding critical thinking in the curriculum so that students will have something to think *about*.

> In projects that focus on problem solving, students have to make informed judgments to choose from an array of possible solutions.

That recommendation reflects best practices in Project Based Learning, which puts academic content and application of 21st century competencies — including critical thinking — at the heart of project design. In projects that focus on problem solving, as most do, students have to make informed judgments to choose from an array of possible solutions. When the subject matter is "problematized," as Case puts it, there is more than one plausible or correct answer. That means students have to think critically to arrive at, and explain their reasons for, their solutions or conclusions.

During projects, students are applying critical thinking when they recognize and define problems worth solving. Critical thinking comes into play when they pose relevant questions, or closely examine a text (which can mean written materials, videos, and other forms of expression), and ascertain the author's perspective. They are thinking critically when they evaluate information and draw on credible sources to support an argument. Students demonstrate critical thinking again when they show that they understand academic vocabulary (such as hypothesis, causation, or evidence) and are able to use such terms with precision to talk about what they have learned as a result of their in-depth inquiry.

Classroom Look-fors

Critical Thinking: What should you see?

During a classroom visit, what should you look for if you want to know that students are developing their capacity to think critically? If you are a school leader doing a classroom walk-through, instructional coach offering feedback on PBL practices, or colleague providing peer critique, look for evidence that students are being given opportunities to think critically. How often do you see students:

- Compare information from different sources before completing a task or an assignment?

- Draw their own conclusions based on analysis of data, facts, or relevant information?

- Summarize or create their own interpretation of what they have read or been taught?

- Analyze competing arguments, perspectives, or solutions to a problem?

- Develop a persuasive argument based on supporting evidence or reasoning?

- Try to solve complex problems or answer questions that have no single correct answer or solution?

These questions can be useful for reflecting on your own practice, too. Ask yourself how often you hear students questioning the reliability of source material (for example, what they find on the Internet). Are students able to draw their own conclusions, based on evidence, or are they more apt to echo others' opinions? Do you provide students with examples of people who think critically to address current problems? How else might you model and encourage the kind of thinking you want to see in your students?

Project Spotlight: Campaign Ad Project

Although most high school juniors and seniors are not yet old enough to vote, students have demonstrated in an interdisciplinary project that they know what it means to think critically about hot-button political issues. The Campaign Ad Project — a perennial favorite during election years — challenges student teams to evaluate the pros and cons of current ballot measures, take a position on one of them, and then develop their own political advertisements to influence specific voter audiences.

First introduced at Sir Francis Drake High in San Anselmo, California, the project has been adopted by Metropolitan Arts and Technology High School in San Francisco to teach critical thinking and help students master important academic content. Bob Lenz, a former teacher at Drake and co-founder and CEO of Envision Schools (which includes Metro), explains the value of having students answer this Driving Question: *What is the most effective persuasive technique used by the media to "tip" voters' minds?* "The Campaign Ad Project serves as a powerful tool for students to engage in the election," Lenz explains, "especially since some will be voting for the first time and the rest will soon officially join our political process. It also provides relevance for the study of U.S. History, Government and/or English" (Lenz, 2012). He credits teachers Justin Wells and Abby Benedetto with developing and updating the project to keep it fresh over several election seasons.

> The kickoff conversation sets the stage for an in-depth investigation into government, media literacy, and video production.

Launching the project

To get the project off to a fast start, teachers screen grainy, black-and-white television ads that first aired before students — or even their parents — were born. The jingles and low-tech graphics may seem quaint or corny at first, but they get students curious about how TV advertisements have shaped the course of history. To make the project more personal, teachers remind students that they are about to become voters themselves. How will they cut through the hype and media manipulation to decide what they really think about the important issues they will face at the ballot box? That kickoff conversation sets the stage for an in-depth investigation into government, media literacy, and video production. Students undertake several smaller assignments en route to their final product: a TV ad designed to sway today's voters about a specific state ballot issue. Here's how English teacher Abby Benedetto explained the culminating product to her students before the 2012 election (emphasis has been added to point out the many critical thinking opportunities in this project):

*You have spent the past several months **taking a hard look at how the media employs persuasive techniques in targeted ways** to try and change the public's mind about people and issues. At the same time, we have been reading about the **critical factors that help to "tip" ideas, products, and movements** from just a fad to a trend or an epidemic. You must now **synthesize all of that learning into an argumentative essay** that lays out **your best analysis of the most powerful persuasive technique**, and the effect it can have.*

*You will **incorporate evidence** from multiple media advertisements, any of the articles we have read in class, as well as excerpts from Malcolm Gladwell's The Tipping Point to **support your claim**. This argumentative essay will serve as **your endorsement of the most powerful persuasive technique** used in written or visual communication.*

*Your job is to **think critically about the various persuasive techniques** that you saw used in this campaign by the media as well as what your group used in your own campaign ad. You will **identify what you believe to be the most effective technique**, and **support why it is effective** and what result it had on the campaign and the public. You will then **draw connections** between this technique and its effects to one of the three rules of The Tipping Point in order to **make conclusions** about how that persuasive technique could cause a campaign to "tip."*

The Campaign Ad Project teaches students to evaluate information, recognize media bias, and construct and communicate their own well-reasoned arguments.

Building knowledge and skills

Along with serving the real-world goal of preparing students to be informed voters and engaged citizens, the Campaign Ad Project teaches students to evaluate information, recognize media bias, and construct and communicate their own well-reasoned arguments. By asking students to apply critical thinking to produce something new, the project gives them reason to put their understanding to work.

Early in the project, as students critically analyze political advertising from previous eras, they discuss questions such as: Who were the backers and creators of various ad campaigns? What was their interest in the issue? What techniques did they use to influence voters? What information was omitted from their message? These conversations probe beyond the surface, helping students look for different perspectives, analyze attempts to manipulate audiences, and detect bias in media messages. At the same time, students are evaluating the effectiveness of advertising techniques that might prove effective when it is time to make their own ads for the culminating event.

Students also have to think critically to determine which side of an issue they will support. Working in teams, each focusing on a different ballot proposition, students must reach consensus about what position their team will take. Reaching consensus involves making convincing arguments, supported by evidence, and also listening closely to counter arguments offered by peers who disagree with their position.

To encourage students to consider diverse perspectives, teachers have teams interview individuals and focus groups of potential voters. Using the same strategies political scientists use to understand and influence voters, students use information they gather from interviews to inform the content and approach of their own political ads.

> Students ask viewers, "Have our advertisements persuaded you how to vote on this issue at the polls tomorrow?"

Developing products

Students know from the start that the project will conclude with the creation of original political advertisements to share with a live audience. Before moving into video production, however, teams work through a series of milestone assignments involving research, analysis, and writing. They also analyze campaign ads developed by previous classes.

When students are ready to develop their own final products, they start with scripts and storyboards. Peer feedback at this early stage helps them improve their creative plans. By the time they pick up video cameras, select music, and start editing footage, they have a clear vision of what they want to produce and why it will meet their goals as a persuasive ad. More peer feedback at the rough cut stage helps students fine-tune their final products.

Presenting products

At their culminating event on election eve, students screen their videos during a public showcase in the evening. The audience includes parents and other prospective voters — representatives of the very demographic groups that students intend to influence with their persuasive advertisements. To prepare viewers for this event, students write program notes that include an objective description of the proposition they have chosen to promote or counter. Feedback from the audience helps students assess their performance as media creators. They ask viewers, "Have our advertisements persuaded you how to vote on this issue at the polls tomorrow?" Later, students reflect on this authentic feedback in their project debrief.

At the conclusion of one Campaign Ad Project, teacher Justin Wells reflected in a video interview about the growth in critical thinking he saw emerge through the project. One student, for example, came away with an expanded "sense of himself as an intellectual," as a result of the ideas he contributed to his team. Another, whose personal opinions were often at odds with his peers, was able to convey his thinking in a respectful way which caused other students to listen and defend their positions. A team of teenage boys had to think hard about how to appeal to the specific voter demographic they decided to sway: middle-aged women. After conducting interviews with members of this demographic and recognizing that pocketbook issues mattered most in their decision making, students decided to tailor their ad to make an economic argument rather than an emotional one. (See an archive of the project at **teacher.justinwells.net**). Listen to Justin Wells reflect on the project in videos at **pearsonschool.com**.

Bulletin Board

Research Spotlight:
PBL Teachers Scaffold Critical Thinking

Getting good at critical thinking takes practice and reinforcement of key habits, such as consulting and comparing multiple sources before completing an assignment. Teachers who use PBL are almost twice as likely (50 percent of PBL teachers versus 26 percent of non-PBL teachers) to ask their students to compare information from multiple sources. Students also need practice in analyzing competing arguments or perspectives. Again, this is more likely to happen in PBL settings: 63% of teachers who use PBL ask students to do this at least once a week, while only 42% of teachers who do not use PBL do this weekly.

Source: Hixson, Ravitz, and Whisman, 2012

Your Turn: Design, Develop, and Determine

To teach and assess critical thinking in PBL, use a three-part approach:

Design

Every project should challenge students to think. Certain types of projects and Driving Questions, however, are especially well-suited to helping students develop and become proficient in critical thinking and problem solving. The Campaign Ad Project, for instance, made it clear from the outset that students would need to evaluate evidence and make a defensible argument of their own.

At the project design stage, consider how the Driving Question itself will set the stage for teaching and reinforcing critical thinking. Roland Case (2012) suggests framing Driving Questions so that they encourage students to make evaluations. For example, use key words like "best" or "most effective." For example, "What was the most effective New Deal program?" and "What is the best way to improve traffic flow around our school?" Or end the question with a "so that…" phrase, emphasizing the criteria or specifications students need to address. For example, "How can we choose the best restaurants for our school food court *so that* all the needs of students are met?" Or, "How can we design our creek clean-up effort *so that* we provide the greatest benefits for wildlife?"

On the other hand, steer clear of questions that focus on determining criteria but fall short of applying them. For example, reword "What are the qualities of a hero?" to ask, "How can I honor the heroes who have most shaped my life?" Instead of asking, "What should we consider when deciding how to pay for college?" ask, "How can mathematical modeling help us plan the best strategy for avoiding heavy college debt?"

Word questions so that they prompt students to make judgments. For example, a Driving Question might ask, "Was Harry Truman a war criminal?" Deciding that someone is a war criminal means judging whether the person was responsible for horrific acts that violated fundamental human rights (Case, 2012).

Consider these examples of the types of projects that emphasize critical thinking:

Mock trial or debate projects challenge students to present evidence in support of arguments and also anticipate (and respond to) counter arguments. Driving Questions might ask:

- How would we advise the Supreme Court to rule on the Affordable Care Act?

- What are the limits to free speech?

- Was Mohammed Ali guilty of being anti-American?

- Can DNA evidence be trusted in criminal trials?

Scientific investigations challenge students to make predictions or hypotheses, gather and analyze data, and explain cause-and-effect relationships in a system. Driving Questions might ask:

- What is the best way to keep pollutants from our school parking lot out of the creek at our neighborhood park?

- How can we prevent polar bears from going the way of the Dodo?

- Will climate change end the great American road trip?

Interpreting events from the past or from literature challenges students to evaluate source material, make connections, and represent divergent points of view. Driving Questions might ask:

- What is the best way for us to honor the forgotten Nisei Soldier heroes from our community?

> Word Driving Questions so that they prompt students to make judgments.

- Which contemporary authors reflect the experiences of my family?

- How can our county historical museum update exhibits so that we attract younger audiences?

- What does *Cyrano de Bergerac* tell us about the need to be yourself?

Design challenges ask students to develop original solutions that meet specific criteria. For example:

- How can we prevent bike-car collisions without requiring new funding for traffic safety?

- How can we increase the thrill of a roller-coaster ride without making it too risky?

- How can we design emergency housing for disaster victims so that it is inexpensive, easy to transport, and quick to install?

Develop

If critical thinking is a term that's unfamiliar or unclear to students, help them define what this means in their own words. Encourage them to be on the lookout for examples of critical thinking at work, in their own lives, and in politics, entertainment, or current events. Use the following guidelines to help you teach students what critical thinking means and what it looks like in practice.

> If critical thinking is a term that's unfamiliar or unclear to students, help them define what this means in their own words.

Build on students' experiences

For starters, you might ask students to describe occasions when they have had to make a choice or decision. Did they compare the pros and cons of different options? Did they think about the potential consequences of their choice? Were they influenced by others' opinions? How did they know whose advice they could trust? Did their own assumptions help or hinder their thinking process? What helped them arrive at a decision? Help students recognize the subtle difference between making a decision and doing the critical thinking that provides a basis for making a decision. When students offer examples of decisions in their lives, follow up by asking, How do you know this was a good decision? You might share a humorous film or video clip of people engaged in an argument (TV sitcoms and talk shows are rich sources). Ask students if the characters are backing up their positions with evidence (and it is reliable?). Are they using persuasive language? Or are they simply trying to out-shout the other person?

Bulletin Board — Coming to Terms with Critical Thinking

Various organizations have developed their own definitions of critical thinking. Here are a few:

Partnership for 21st Century Skills	The ability to make effective judgments based on evidence, to make connections between ideas, to reflect on learning experiences, and to evaluate potential solutions to critical issues
Common Core State Standards	Students can, without significant scaffolding, comprehend and evaluate complex texts across a range of types and disciplines, and they can construct effective arguments and convey intricate or multifaceted information
Foundation for Critical Thinking	The mode of thinking in which the thinker improves the quality of his or her thinking by skillfully analyzing it... its purpose, as well as its information, inferences(s), assumptions, implications, main concept(s), and point of view
The Critical Thinking Consortium	A person is thinking critically — making a reasoned judgment — when she attempts to assess or judge the merits of possible options in light of relevant factors or criteria

Help students understand what it looks like

As a class activity, have students unpack widely adopted definitions of critical thinking. Make sure they understand key vocabulary and can explain how they would put these concepts to work. (Point out that doing a close reading of text — or any media — is one of the hallmarks of a critical thinker.)

Make sure students can explain critical thinking in their own words. For example, they might define making an effective argument as: "I can back up my position with reliable evidence." Ask them to think more critically by also defining what they mean by "reliable evidence."

When you introduce projects, help students recognize opportunities to develop and apply critical thinking. In the Campaign Ad Project, when teacher Abby Benedetto explained the culminating product, she was specific about the kind of thinking and type of evidence she was expecting from students.

Anticipate critical thinking opportunities

Between the Entry Event that launches a project and the showcase that celebrates its conclusion, students will encounter a number of situations that call on them to think critically. Consider how much previous experience students have had with projects or assignments that asked for critical thinking. If this is new ground, be deliberate about breaking down aspects of critical thinking into accessible activities that you reinforce through practice. For example, you may want to introduce activities that ask students to compare/contrast, identify bias, or make inferences. Help them see that thinking critically becomes a habit when you consistently ask certain kinds of questions.

> Thinking critically becomes a habit when you consistently ask certain kinds of questions.

By anticipating the critical thinking opportunities of a project such as the ones listed below, you can plan to teach and support the competencies that you know students will need (or will need to improve upon). Fine-tune projects so that you are continuing to build students' critical thinking capacities. Make sure they recognize their growth. After all, critical thinkers make a habit of thinking about their own thinking!

- **Understanding the problem:** Remind students that thoroughly understanding a problem or question is an important aspect of critical thinking. After introducing the Driving Question (or co-writing it with students), make sure the Need to Know discussion prompts students to think about the criteria that they are expected to meet. If the Driving Question asks students to choose the "best" solution to keep pollutants out of the school parking lot, for instance, does "best" mean measurable improvement, most affordable, most sustainable, or something else? Help students think about what they need to know when it comes to criteria or standards implied by the Driving Question.

- **Engaging with text:** When you know that a project will involve difficult reading material, help students think critically about the text by planning activities such as Socratic Seminars, concept mapping, or guided reading (for suggestions, see below: *More Tools for Better Thinkers*). For example, in the Campaign Ad Project, students had to analyze propositions on the upcoming ballot. This required them to closely read the Voter's Pamphlet to understand complex issues, identify points of view, point out factual contradictions, and make sense of technical vocabulary. By engaging with the Voter's Pamphlet as "text," students were also meeting Common Core expectations to develop proficiency as readers of nonfiction.

  To prepare students for a class discussion about a challenging reading, you might have them annotate a text with sticky notes highlighting key ideas, along with their questions and reactions. You can use either the paper variety or online notes that students can share using a social bookmarking tool like Diigo. For English learners who are new to Socratic seminars, provide sentence frames to help organize their responses to the text. (For example: "I agree with what the author is saying here because_____.")

If readings contain unfamiliar vocabulary, incorporate strategies to help students build their understanding of new terms. For example, students might create a collaborative glossary or build a word wall for quick reference. You might use multimedia materials to provide students with additional context or background information to support their learning. You might provide English learners with concept maps that are partially or completely filled out to scaffold their understanding of difficult text.

- **Understanding perspective.** To help students understand issues from diverse perspectives, have them role-play scenarios to develop better insights into specific points of view or conduct interviews or surveys with people whose point of view differs from their own. In the Campaign Ad Project, students conducted focus groups with potential voters to understand their perspectives.

> To help students understand issues from diverse perspectives, have them role-play scenarios to develop better insights into specific points of view.

- **Reaching consensus:** If students need to arrive at consensus, as they did in Campaign Ad Project, help them bring their critical thinking to this task. For example, they might develop guidelines for reaching consensus, such as, "Don't just listen to the loudest voice in the room," or, "Weigh pros and cons—don't just count them." This naturally overlaps with encouraging effective collaboration (which will be discussed in detail in Chapter 3). To emphasize the critical thinking aspects, you might plan a fishbowl-style demonstration of a process for shared decision making. In modeling the process, help students think critically about why it's important for everyone to contribute ideas, listen to what others have to say, evaluate suggestions as a group, and build buy-in so that everyone on the team is able to support the final decision.

Troubleshoot critical thinking challenges

Formative assessment will give you important feedback about students' progress as critical thinkers throughout a project. Based on informal discussions with students, observations of student teams, questions students ask on exit slips or raise in reflections, and other formative check-ins, you will spot more opportunities to emphasize or support critical thinking, or troubleshoot challenges. Make adjustments in your Project Calendar to address these just-in-time learning needs so that students can get to deeper thinking.

Bulletin Board | Building Information Literacy

When students are doing research, remind them to look for bias and consider the validity of information. Inquiry may lead students to consider a wide range of information sources, both online and in print. Encourage students to turn a critical eye on all kinds of content, including text, videos, photos, and other sources.

Ask critical questions. In an essay about teaching critical thinking, Robert Swartz of the National Center for Teaching Thinking suggests questions worth asking about all kinds of information:

- What is the author or creator trying to convince me of?
- What reasons are offered to support this?
- Is there anything not stated that the author assumes that also serves as a reason?
- Are there missing counterarguments or unspoken disadvantages?
- Is there missing information? What else would I need to know to be convinced by this argument?
- Is the information provided reliable? (How can you tell?)
- Does the author or creator demonstrate sound reasoning? What makes you say so?

Encourage media literacy. Media literacy expert Renee Hobbs suggests asking students to consider three key questions to encourage critical evaluation of media:

- Who's the author?
- What's the purpose of this message?
- How was this message constructed?

Consider the (online) source. When students are assessing online sources for authority and validity, teach them to consider what the Center for News Literacy (**centerfornewsliteracy.org**) calls "currency." Help students evaluate whether information is trustworthy by asking:

- Does the website have recent or updated information?
- Are the links still live?
- Is the organization that published the information still in business?

For example:

If you overhear students making faulty arguments, that's your signal to address conceptual misunderstandings with a mini-lesson or whole-class discussion. Ask students to explain the difference between arguments based on logic versus emotion. Make sure they know how to support arguments with evidence, and that they can demonstrate the validity of source material.

If you see students relying on weak sources, send them back to the research drawing board. This may be time for a mini-lesson on information literacy or a good opportunity to have them consult with a school librarian or media specialist to improve their search results.

If students are critical of the direction their project is going, probe deeper to find out why. Perhaps their team consulted with an expert who pointed out counter-arguments to their ideas or suggested unintended consequences they didn't anticipate. Or perhaps their product is too complicated, or their proposed solution to a problem is not going to meet criteria, or they're not considering their audience properly. To help them get back on track, you might schedule a team meeting to help them consider alternative solutions. Encourage them to ask classmates for help thinking critically about how to respond to counter-arguments.

More Tools for Better Thinkers

Your PBL toolkit should include a range of classroom routines and teaching tools so that you can support your students on their way to becoming better critical thinkers. Here are some examples, along with suggestions for when and how you might use them during a project.

THINKING MAPS

How can you tell if students are thinking critically? It can be hard to know what's going on inside their heads. Concept maps and other graphic organizers make students' thinking visible and can be especially helpful for English learners. By enabling students to capture their ideas succinctly, in an organized way, these tools set the stage for more productive conversations that take thinking deeper. Robert Swartz of the National Center for Teaching Thinking explains that, by using graphic organizers, students have a place to record their thoughts (for example, while they are reading a text), and can find and articulate these ideas later, in class discussions.

- **When:** Use thinking maps when students are reading a challenging text, doing research, and engaging in other learning activities that introduce them to unfamiliar information.

- **How:** Use thinking maps to help students think about:
  - ▸ Cause-and-effect relationships in a system (for example: showing the factors leading up to an economic crisis)
  - ▸ Comparing and contrasting (for example: listing pros and cons for a proposal or comparing the qualities of two pieces of art)
  - ▸ Evidence to support an argument (for example: extracting key ideas from a speech or data from a newspaper article)
  - ▸ Relationship of parts to the whole (for example: showing how an animal relates to its ecosystem)

Socratic seminars encourage participants to actively engage with each other in critical thinking, listening, and dialogue

SOCRATIC SEMINARS

Socratic seminars encourage participants to actively engage with each other in critical thinking, listening, and dialogue about a common text, video, or other source of information.

- **When:** Use this activity when students are building knowledge for the project (for example, after they have completed a shared reading assignment or are comparing source documents).

- **How:** To prepare for a seminar, students first examine the source material closely. Have them make notes, highlight key passages, or record questions that occur to them while engaging with the material. Differentiate instruction by supporting struggling readers or English learners with guided reading strategies, as needed.

  Assign specific roles to keep the seminar moving along: A discussion director asks the opening question and keeps the conversation focused. A timekeeper monitors the clock and makes sure all participants have opportunities to speak. A scribe or note-taker creates a record of the dialogue.

  For students who are new to this approach, it may take role-play or norm-setting to get used to these roles. For example, group norms might encourage participants to speak respectfully, listen to fellow participants, and wait their turn to speak. Comments should reference the text (or whatever source material is being discussed), rather than airing personal opinions. Model how to be an effective discussion director before asking students to take on this role.

  (More information about conducting Socratic seminars, including sample lesson plans, is available online from ReadWriteThink at **readwritethink.org**.

Connect/Extend/Challenge

A protocol developed by Project Zero, Connect/Extend/Challenge encourages students to build on what they know.

- **When:** Use this protocol when students are developing their own ideas or making sense of information that is new or unfamiliar.

- **How:** Use discussion prompts that ask students to:
  - *Connect:* How are the ideas and information presented CONNECTED to what you already knew?
  - *Extend:* What new ideas did you get that EXTENDED or pushed your thinking in new directions?
  - *Challenge:* What is still CHALLENGING or confusing for you to get your mind around? What questions, wonderings, or puzzles do you now have?

TIP FROM THE **CLASSROOM**

Use Discussion Prompts

Model and reinforce critical thinking during seminar discussions by teaching students how to frame their comments. At KIPP King Collegiate High School in San Lorenzo, California, students learn to use these phrases to shape their conversations during Socratic seminars (Edutopia, 2011):

Paraphrasing:
- So you are saying that...
- In other words, you think...
- What I hear you saying is...

Acknowledging Ideas:
- My idea is similar to yours in that...
- I agree with (a person) that...
- My idea builds upon _____'s idea...

Affirming:
- That's an interesting idea.
- I hadn't thought of that before.
- I see what you mean.

Soliciting a Response:
- What do you think?
- We haven't heard from you yet.
- Do you agree?
- What answer did you get?

Asking for Clarification:
- What do you mean?
- Will you explain that again?
- I have a question about that.

Disagreeing:
- I don't agree with you because...
- I got a different answer than you because...
- I see it a different way because...

(For an alternative to Socratic seminars, see the description of Café Conversations in Chapter 4, page 72.)

Determine

At the end of the project, you will manage students' demonstrations of learning and determine how they have progressed as critical thinkers. At the culminating event, take advantage of opportunities to have students explain the role that critical thinking played in their work. You could, for example, ask students to give three examples of how and when they used critical thinking, and how it improved their efforts.

If students are sharing their work with a live audience or expert judges, set the stage for the audience to ask follow-up questions, perhaps questioning their evidence or challenging students' conclusions. Encourage viewers to ask about the reliability of sources that students consulted, or whether students' own assumptions were challenged in the course of the project. For example, a project in which students interviewed Vietnam War veterans led students to reconsider their previous opinions about America's role in the conflict.

The project culmination is also the time to put your summative assessment plan into action. Earlier in the project, you provided students with a rubric or scoring guide that describes quality thinking in student-friendly language. Ideally, you have been referring to this rubric throughout the project — not just at the end. Now, use it to evaluate students' final products or their project journals for clear evidence of critical thinking. (See **Useful Stuff** for sample rubric.)

Bulletin Board ## Thoughts on Critical Thinking

You want students to read like a detective, write like an investigative reporter.
— **David Coleman, co-author of CCSS ELA**

Neither children nor adults acquire critical thinking skills about mass media, popular culture, or digital media just by using technology tools themselves.
— **Renee Hobbs, founder of Media Education Lab**

Thinking without content is vacuous, and content acquired without thought is mindless and inert.
— **Roland Case, co-founder,
The Critical Thinking Consortium**

Early adulthood presents a multitude of quandaries and challenges that cry out for evaluative thinking... issues; products; new ideas; and people. In addition, young adults urgently need the ability to evaluate opportunities (... job offers... graduate school, or deciding whether to stay out late partying the night before an important job interview).

— **Mel Levine, Professor of Pediatrics**

Remember to reflect

Although reflection is an essential element in all projects, it's especially important for helping students think about their own thinking. Use reflection to prompt students to take stock of their habits of mind as critical thinkers. For example, you might ask them: How confident are you when you have to back up an argument? Or: How has your thinking (about a particular issue) changed as a result of this project? What has influenced your thinking? See **Useful Stuff** for more reflection prompts.

TECH TIP Tools for Critical Thinking

A variety of technology tools and online resources are available to help students organize and share their thinking. Here are a few to consider incorporating into PBL:

Concept mapping: Online tools such as MindMeister (**mindmeister.com**) and Mindomo (**mindomo.com**) enable students to create, share, and comment on concept maps. Use concept maps to help students diagram their understanding of concepts such as parts-to-whole or compare-and-contrast.

Cause and effect: Seeing Reason, a free online tool from Intel (**intel.com**), prompts students think about cause-and-effect relationships in complex systems. The website includes project examples and instructional strategies.

Pros and cons: ProCon, maintained by the independent nonprofit of the same name (**procon.org**), is useful for helping students consider both sides of controversial topics. Factual information on hot-button issues—such as drinking age, teacher tenure, and government bailout of the auto industry—is presented in a nonpartisan format.

Critical Thinking Throughout a Project

with Common Core Alignment

Launching the Project

An engaging Entry Event and open-ended Driving Question launch students on their inquiry experience. Need to Know discussions raise questions that will guide students' investigation.

▶ Students analyze the Driving Question and project tasks to identify what they need to know, and consider the various points of view that might exist on the topic of investigation.

▶ Students ask questions that focus or broaden the inquiry. (CC ELA.6-12.W.7)

Building Knowledge, Understanding and Skills

Students learn necessary content knowledge from the teacher, readings, and other resources, and gain skills that will help them create project products and answer the Driving Question. They do research, test hypotheses, and gather and analyze data.

▶ Students integrate multiple sources of information to address the Driving Question. (CC ELA.6,11-12.RI.7))

▶ Students assess the credibility, accuracy, and usefulness of each source of information. They decide if information is relevant and sufficient. (CC ELA.6-12.W.8)

▶ Students evaluate a speaker's point of view, reasoning, and use of evidence and rhetoric. (CC ELA.6-12.SL.3)

Developing and Revising Ideas and Products

Students consider diverse perspectives and generate multiple solutions, designs, and answers to the Driving Question. Through cycles of critical feedback, they refine their thinking and improve on early ideas as they create final products.

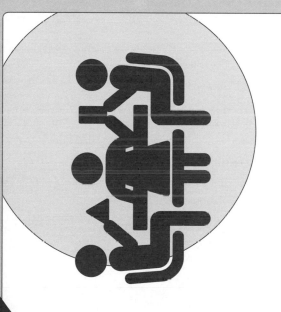

▲ Students evaluate arguments for possible answers to the Driving Question by assessing whether reasoning is valid and evidence is relevant and sufficient.(CC ELA 6-12.SL.3,RI.8; 6-12 Math Practices.3)

▲ Students justify their choice of criteria used to evaluate product drafts. Students revise inadequate product drafts, designs or solutions and explain why they will better meet evaluation criteria. (CC ELA.6-12.W.5)

▲ Students craft arguments to support claims using valid reasoning and relevant and sufficient evidence. (CC ELA.Math.6-12. W1, WHST.1; Math 6-12 Math Practices.3)

Presenting Products and Answers to Driving Questions

Students share the results of their efforts with a public audience, demonstrating what they learned in the project. They explain and defend their research, product design, and strategies for problem solving. Finally, they reflect on their experience.

▲ Students evaluate the advantages and disadvantages of using different mediums to present a particular idea or topic. (CC ELA.8.RI.7)

▲ Students recognize the limitations of their answer to the Driving Question or product design and consider alternative perspectives. (CC ELA 11-12.SL.4)

▲ Students justify their conclusions. (CC Math.6-12 Math Practices.3)

▲ Students present information such that listeners can follow the line of reasoning. (CC ELA.9-12.SL.4)

37

Bulletin Board — Thoughts on Collaboration

Collaboration is the amplification you get by connecting up human beings who are listening, interested, bring separate depth to the problem, bring breadth that gives them interest in the entire solution, and [are able to] communicate on multiple levels.

— Randy Nelson, dean of Pixar University

Chance favors the connected mind.

—Steven Johnson, author

Most great learning happens in groups. Collaboration is the stuff of growth.

—Sir Ken Robinson, author and speaker

Employees who are poor team players… are just a pink slip away from losing their jobs.

— Deborah Hildebrand, business writer

If people knew how to collaborate well, the world would simply work better.

— Morten Hansen, researcher and author

COLLABORATION IN PBL

When students in Roxbury, Massachusetts, are nearing the end of sixth grade, they spend several weeks on a project that involves navigating Boston Harbor and the Charles River aboard wooden rowing boats. Academic content is thoughtfully integrated, such as investigations into local geography and the science of waves and currents. Students take on fitness challenges, as well. Equally important is the goal of building community. Students literally have to pull together to maneuver their vessels. Learning firsthand about teamwork and collaboration gets students ready to navigate the looming challenges of middle school and high school.

Why Emphasize Teamwork?

Learning to collaborate serves students well, not only in school but for years to come. Today's workplace requires more collaboration than ever before. That's true in traditional occupations as well as newer fields. Teamwork is standard practice for everyone from nurses to construction crews to call center operators.

On a more global scale, it's easy to see that many of today's problems are too big and multifaceted for any individual to tackle alone. Experts who are highly specialized in one area need to be able to work with peers across disciplines to address all aspects of a problem. Virtual tools enable teams to collaborate across distances and time zones. That means team members need to know how to navigate cultural differences and use technology tools effectively. Increasingly, innovation and problem solving result from team efforts rather than through the work of solitary inventors. Across all sectors — from medicine to movie-making to marketing — effective teams accomplish better results than their members could achieve by working alone.

To get a better idea of how to teach students to collaborate, let's take a look at one project that transformed the learning culture of a whole school. The same project idea could also work in a single classroom or across a grade level.

Collaboration and the Common Core

Embedded in the Common Core State Standards are expectations that, over time, students will become increasingly skilled at teamwork and collaboration. As students progress from grades 6-12, the standards call on them to develop proficiency as collaborators through small-group discussions, peer review experiences, and other activities that help them appreciate and build on others' ideas. By the time they complete high school, students should be able to exchange diverse ideas and work together to engage in civil, democratic decision making. (CC 11-12.SL.1b)

Speaking and listening standards for English Language Arts, for example, call on middle and high school students to:

▶ Engage effectively in a range of collaborative discussions (one-on-one, in groups, and teacher-led) with diverse partners [on grade level topics], building on others' ideas and expressing their own clearly. (CC 6-12.SL.1)

By grade 8, a student should be able to:

▶ Follow rules for collegial discussions and decision-making, track progress toward specific goals and deadlines, and define individual roles as needed. (CC 8.SL.1b)

By grades 11 and 12, students should be able to:

▶ Initiate and participate effectively in a range of collaborative discussions (one-on-one, in groups, and teacher-led) with diverse partners, building on others' ideas and expressing their own clearly and persuasively. (CC 11-12.SL.1a)

With increased proficiency as communicators, upper-level high school students should be able to:

▶ Propel conversations by posing and responding to questions that probe reasoning and evidence; ensure a hearing for a full range of positions on a topic or issue; clarify, verify, or challenge ideas and conclusions; and promote divergent and creative perspectives. (CC 11-12.SL.1c)

Writing standards emphasize the importance of learning to use technology tools to foster collaboration. For example, students should be able to:

▶ Use technology, including the Internet, to produce and publish writing and present the relationships between information and ideas efficiently as well as to interact and collaborate with others. (CC 6-12.W.6)

PBL helps students build their collaboration toolkit by putting them into situations that require authentic teamwork, along with necessary supports to help them succeed in team situations. Although the academic content that students learn and the products they produce will vary from one project to the next, the collaboration skills they learn through PBL are evergreen.

For students who are accustomed to working solo on more traditional class assignments, it can take some adjusting to get used to accepting shared accountability for team efforts. Students may need your help learning to work with classmates of diverse backgrounds, abilities, and perspectives. It may take role-modeling and reflection for them to recognize that effective teamwork involves capitalizing on others' strengths as well as using their own talents. If they are new to collaboration, they will benefit from explicit instruction in how to give and receive feedback that is tactful and constructive. An emphasis on teaching students to be productive team members builds the collaborative culture that will help them succeed in PBL—and in life. (See related Bulletin Board: Explaining Teamwork to Students and Parents, page 47.)

Project Spotlight: Project Lion Pride

Students at Howe High School in rural Oklahoma didn't have much prior experience with PBL when they embarked on Project Lion Pride. Yet the schoolwide project managed to engage all 167 students, from grades 9-12, with the compelling Driving Question: *How can we make our school better?* In nine weeks, student teams not only generated a slate of creative ideas to improve their campus and enhance their school culture but also secured community support to make improvements a reality.

Project Lion Pride wouldn't have been such a success without collaboration by both teachers and students. "It's been transformational," said Tammy Parks, district technology coach and also the broadcast journalism teacher at the high school. Before introducing the project, the school was already well along with a 1:1 laptop initiative that made technology ubiquitous. Teachers had taken part in PBL workshops, but most instruction still tended to be traditional rather than project based. Project Lion Pride was intended to help both teachers and students get more familiar with PBL and, specifically, help them get better at working collaboratively.

Teachers invested professional development time to design the project together. "It was a bonding experience for us," Park reflected. "As a staff of 13 teachers, we modeled teamwork for our students. We were definitely in this together."

Launching the project

To launch Project Lion Pride, the entire Howe High student body assembled for an Entry Event in an historic school auditorium that recently had been renovated. For most students, this was their first chance to see the restored space. On stage were two alumni. They talked about the school's role as the heart of their small community and why they take such pride in being Howe graduates. Then students were sent off on a campus scavenger hunt. Using video cameras that the school provided or their own cell phones, they took pictures and shot video of the spots on campus that cause them to feel pride. All this "evidence" of pride was gathered digitally, using a collaborative Web 2.0 tool called Posterous (**posterous.com**).

Classroom Look-fors

Collaboration:
What should you see?

During a classroom visit, what should you look for if you want to know that students are developing their collaboration capabilities? If you are a school leader doing a classroom walk-through, instructional coach offering feedback on PBL practices, or colleague providing peer critique, look for evidence that students are being given opportunities to develop their abilities as collaborators. How often do you see students:

■ Work in pairs or small groups to complete a task together?

■ Work with other students to set goals and create a plan for their team?

■ Create joint products using contributions from each student?

■ Present their group work to the class, teacher, or others?

■ Work as a team to incorporate feedback on group tasks or products?

■ Give feedback to peers or assess other students' work?

These questions can be useful for reflecting on your own practice, too. If you notice that students struggle with some team activities, confuse leadership with being bossy, or have trouble coming to consensus around shared goals, think about additional steps you might take to build a classroom culture that fosters collaboration and shared decision making.

"We compiled everything they posted and played it back for them the next day," Parks explained. "We said, 'Here's what the school looks like to you now. What if you had $1,000 to make it better? What would you do?'" At that point, students were introduced to their team members and met with their assigned teacher to learn more about the project.

Building knowledge and skills

Students' first exercise in collaboration was to choose a team name and design a team banner. This low-stakes activity also gave the teacher assigned to each team a chance to watch students interact. For example, students had to work together to pick a team name that everyone could support. Later in the project, they would have to reach consensus about higher-stakes decisions. Making a banner together provided another low-stakes opportunity for bonding, complete with glue and glitter, and an outlet for team creativity. "It was the best session for team-building," Parks says. "You could feel the momentum building."

Teachers carefully planned the team assignments in advance, balancing each team with a mix of students from grades 9-12. They avoided putting siblings, close friends, or romantic partners on the same team. Although each team had at least one upperclass student, there was no pre-assigned team leader. Each of the 13 teachers was responsible for managing two teams, with two hours per week dedicated to collaborative "PBL time."

Developing products

The next team challenge was to develop a realistic proposal for school improvement. Teams typically generated many ideas before narrowing their focus to just one suggestion. Reaching consensus required team members to listen respectfully to each other's ideas and think critically about the pros and cons of different proposals. By the time students presented their well-researched team proposal to a panel of judges, they wanted everyone on the team on board and ready to pitch in with enthusiasm.

To research the feasibility and costs of their proposals, students consulted with experts in the community for help with everything from addressing engineering questions to pricing construction materials. Consulting with adults was new for most students. "They've never been in a position to have to call on adults, contact organizations, ask for donations, or negotiate on price," Parks said.

An unexpected outcome was students' newfound understanding of each other's strengths. "Students got to know classmates they don't normally hang around with. As they learned to work together, it led to a climate change across the whole school," Parks observed, "and better understanding of others' learning styles." Students with special needs were valued for their team contributions.

An unexpected outcome was students' newfound understanding of each other's strengths.

Research Snapshot:
PBL Teachers Scaffold Collaboration

Part of being an effective collaborator is being able to make a realistic plan for reaching common goals, tapping everyone's talents for a successful team project. In classrooms where teachers use PBL, students have frequent opportunities to set goals together and create plans for their teams. This happens on a weekly basis for 67% of students in PBL classes; among teachers who do not use PBL, only 27% of students regularly set goals together. On a weekly basis, 79 percent of PBL teachers give students opportunities to do assignments that involve contributions from each student. This happens for only 21 percent of students in classes where teachers make limited use of PBL.

Source: Hixson, Ravitz, and Whisman, 2012

Disciplinary issues were rare during the project, despite the freedom students were given to manage their time and organize their own teams. "We had minimal if not zero discipline issues," Parks says. In fact, students who previously posed behavior challenges "now saw great value in teamwork. They realized they have a voice in their learning." Such student reflections were captured by team members who served as embedded reporters. Using video cameras, they interviewed peers about the project, focusing on a different question each week. A strong theme in students' recorded reflections was their ringing endorsement of "getting a say in our learning."

Presenting products

As the culmination of Project Lion Pride approached, some students admitted feeling nervous about having to present their ideas in front of a panel of judges. Knowing that the top-ranked team proposal would be funded and implemented at the school made the project more authentic, but also increased the pressure to perform well. Students became their own best allies by giving each other feedback to improve their presentations and convince judges to invest real money in their collaboratively developed ideas.

Judges were so impressed by the presentations that they decided to fund two projects. One project will correct a drainage problem that turns the school parking lot into a lake during rainy weather. Students consulted with engineers and secured in-kind donations from paving and gravel companies as part of their community outreach. Another proposal involves repairing an historic school sign and restoring a rock wall at the school entrance that was built in the 1930s by Works Progress Administration artisans. It was the brainchild of a team called "Project Tidy Up," which made a compelling argument about the benefits of small steps — and collaboration — to make a big difference.

Your Turn: Design, Develop, and Determine

To teach and assess collaboration in PBL, use a three-part approach:

Design

At the design stage, when you are identifying which academic standards the project will address, take time to consider whether collaboration is going to be essential for project success. You should be able to explain to students (and curious parents) why you are asking them to collaborate rather than work individually on a specific project. Your reason cannot simply be, "Because if we had 30 individual projects I couldn't manage, grade, and present them all." So, at the design stage, take time to think about your compelling reasons to emphasize collaboration in this project.

For example, in Project Lion Pride, teamwork was a deliberate emphasis of the project because of a schoolwide goal to shift to PBL. Teachers were building a foundation for future project success by giving students an experience that required collaboration. Sometimes, the compelling reason for collaboration has to do with the scope or complexity of the project. To produce a video documentary, for example, team members might need to focus on different aspects of the project, such as primary source research, interviewing, storyboarding, and video editing.

Instead of putting students into teams by default, consider the authentic reasons why you want students to work together. For example, will the project require specialized expertise or roles that several students will need to contribute? Does the scope of the project make it too large, complex, or time-consuming for one student to tackle alone? Will diverse viewpoints or different perspectives add to the richness or value of the project? If a project like this happened outside of school, would it likely involve collaboration? Thinking about these questions at the design stage will help you explain to students (and parents) why it's important for them to work in teams rather than as individuals.

> Instead of putting students into teams by default, consider the authentic reasons why you want students to work together.

Designing projects with teams in mind also gives you an opportunity to emphasize student voice and choice, an essential element of PBL. Give teams some leeway to make decisions about the direction of their project and how they will demonstrate what they have learned, within the constraints you have established in the project plan. (Hint: As a check for incorporating student voice in your design, imagine students' final products. You shouldn't expect to see cookie-cutter products or repetitive presentations if you have given students room to make decisions.)

Have "The Talk"

Here's how one PBL veteran describes "the talk" that he regularly conducts with parents to help them understand the importance of collaboration in PBL:

The first parents we usually hear from are the parents of our best students. They don't understand how their son or daughter has gotten such a low grade. "My son has never gotten a grade below a 90!" And we have to have the talk that, at our school, the students need to learn to work with each other to be successful. And, before long, that "A" student is back to having good grades and has learned to help his group be successful.

Project design is also the time to consider how you will assess student work. Because teamwork is such a major component of PBL, many teachers formally assess how well students collaborate. Your assessment plan should include a rubric that defines what quality collaboration looks like. (See **Useful Stuff** for an example.) Even if you don't plan to grade students on collaboration, you will want to encourage effective teamwork in every project.

You may decide to assess some aspects of the project individually, focusing on academic content mastery, and other parts based on teamwork. For example, you might ask students to write individual research papers about a topic they were responsible for investigating during the project. This allows you to better address individual learning needs and assess individual growth. In the same project, you might ask students to make their final presentation as a team, with all team members expected to participate. In your teaching and learning plan, decide which activities require authentic collaboration, which will be assessed individually, and then design your assessments and grading plan accordingly.

Develop

Students start building a foundation for collaboration as early as the primary grades when they learn to share, make friends, take turns, and treat one another fairly. As students mature socially and cognitively, they become better equipped to recognize and consider other viewpoints, negotiate differences with peers, make critical decisions, set shared goals, and work toward them. They're ready to make the shift from cooperation to genuine collaboration—from groups to teams.

Don't assume that students arrive at middle school or high school knowing how to be effective team members, however. Their earlier school experiences may have emphasized cooperation, sharing, and fairness, but those concepts, while important, are different from the active collaboration called for in high-quality PBL. Cooperation typically means "dividing up the work" to get something

Bulletin Board

Explaining Teamwork to Students and Parents

Be prepared for students to challenge your team assignments. "Why can't I work with my friends?" is a common student refrain. Parents, too, may question why their students are being graded on team efforts rather than solely on individual work. To address these concerns, keep the following in mind:

▶ **Make the workplace connection.**
This is an opportunity to remind students — and parents — that effective teams leverage the talents of individual members. Research from the business world underscores the importance of "smart teams" to solicit diverse perspectives and improve ideas (Woolley & Malone, 2011). For most parents, their workplace and community activities likely involve collaboration. Help them make the connection between what their students are learning now and the expectations they will face in the future.

▶ **Emphasize what students gain.**
Help parents and students understand that an emphasis on teamwork does not come at the expense of individual learning. Having students take on interdependent roles on a team tends to heighten student engagement and improve academic learning (Slavin 1996; Johnson & Johnson, 2009). Compared to traditional instructional methods, students engaged in small-group learning achieve higher grades, retain information longer, and have reduced dropout rates, improved communication and collaboration skills, and a better understanding of professional environments (Vega, 2012).

▶ **Address assessment and grading concerns.**
Sharing your assessment plan with students and parents at the start of the project helps them understand how much of the grade will depend on collaboration. Throughout the project, have students reflect on how the team process is going and be transparent about conflicts or challenges. If you hear from parents that their student is pulling too much of the load, that's a signal to regroup and refocus on what collaboration means and why it's essential for project success. At the end of the project, students should be able to explain to their parents why they received the grade they did for collaboration. "That's real-world accountability," says a teacher who relies on transparency to defuse parent critiques about teamwork.

> Collaboration is not simply about agreement; it is about creation.

done. Collaboration, on the other hand, is not simply about agreement; it is about creation. As Michael Schrage puts it in his book, *Shared Minds*: "...collaboration is the process of shared creation: two or more individuals with complementary skills interacting to create a shared understanding that none had previously possessed or could have come to on their own. Collaboration creates a shared meaning about a process, a product, or an event" (Schrage, 1990).

To develop students' collaboration capabilities throughout a project, anticipate key issues and be ready with additional supports, as needed. Use the following guidelines to help you form teams, build students' collaboration skills, and manage their work together.

Know the territory

Make sure, from the outset, that students understand what collaboration means. Ask them to describe real-life examples of effective teamwork. For instance, get them to think about the many specialized roles that come together to make a feature film or digital game. (A quick scan of the credits can be a good conversation starter.) Ask them to consider why cross-cultural collaboration might be necessary for a medical team working to eradicate disease or a business marketing a product internationally.

Help students see that the team skills they are building relate to real life. Ask guest speakers and parents to talk about how they collaborate in their work or when they get involved in community issues. Point out evidence of collaboration during newsworthy events. Have students brainstorm jobs that typically require teamwork (prompt their thinking by mentioning firefighters, hospital employees, car mechanics, supermarket or department store workers, engineers, lawyers). In fact, challenge students to think of any field — from athletics to public safety to aerospace exploration — that doesn't require a team effort. Even solitary artists and writers eventually team up with gallery owners, publishers, and agents to bring their work to audiences. Some schools that emphasize PBL begin each new school year with students interviewing adults from their community about the role of collaboration in their careers and daily lives.

Start with a plan for forming teams

Have a deliberate strategy for forming teams. In Project Lion Pride, teachers carefully planned the team assignments to balance each team with a mix of students from grades 9-12, and to distribute students with special needs across several teams. In a single-grade or subject-area class, you'll also want to aim for a mix of skills and strengths on teams. Plan to address the needs of English learners, gifted students, and other special-needs students so that everyone can maximize contributions to the team.

The more you know about students' strengths, weaknesses, and interests, the better you can balance teams to ensure that each has a mix of skills. Before making team assignments, you might want to survey students about their self-perceptions of the skills they can contribute to teams. For example, they may have developed skills or work habits from pursuing out-of-school interests or hobbies that will be valuable in PBL. Encourage them to contribute these assets to their teams.

To find out about students' interests, you might use a tech tool like Survey Monkey (surveymonkey.com), Google form, or just paper and pencil to inventory the talents in your classroom. Ask wide-ranging questions to learn about students' talents and interests, such as:

- What languages do you speak at home?

- Do you like to doodle or draw cartoons?

- Have you ever made a video?

- What musical instruments do you play?

- Have you ever organized an event (lemonade stand, car wash, etc.)?

- Which sports or clubs do you participate in outside school?

- Do you like to cook? (Any specialities?)

- Do you have a blog?

- Do you consider yourself a good leader?

- Do you contribute to Fan Fiction (fanfiction.net)?

- Are you a gamer?

Team EL Students Strategically

When thinking about your strategy for assigning English learners to teams, the best approach is to stay flexible and keep the purpose of any team activity in mind, advises BIE's English learner expert Rosanna Mucetti. Her rule of thumb: "If your purpose is related to learning content, then use heterogeneous grouping. If it's language-related, then homogeneous groups work better." Consider assigning students to "study teams" as well as "project teams," adds John McCarthy, member of the BIE National Faculty, as another strategy to differentiate instruction during projects.

As an alternative, you could have students interview each other about their interests and skills they could bring to a team. For example, they could ask each other about leadership skills, artistic ability, technological prowess, research and writing skills, and so on.

Some teachers ask students to apply for spots on specific teams, perhaps by submitting a résumé or letter of application. This causes students to identify the strengths they will bring to the team (or areas they hope to improve upon), and reflect on why they are suited for a particular role. It also gives students experience with the real-world activities of preparing résumés and applying for jobs.

Even though students are assigned to specific teams, that doesn't mean you can't be flexible about regrouping them for day-to-day activities. For example, you may decide to give a mini-lesson that only some students will need to take part in, based on your formative assessment. Or you may want to pull together all the English learners for a specific learning activity, even though they are working on different project teams.

Encourage shared leadership

Rather than having a team select "a leader," have different students take on responsibility for specific tasks within teams. For example, a project that involves giving a local business a make-over might have one student assigned to oversee architectural designs for a remodel, another taking the lead on a marketing plan, and another researching sustainability practices to "green" the enterprise. To build everyone's leadership abilities, make sure each student takes on a lead role that's critical for the team's success. Help students understand that taking the lead on a task doesn't mean doing it all by yourself, but rather bringing out the best in your fellow team members. As a project management strategy, you might ask teams to identify a point person who will be your main contact for communicating about project logistics or delivering progress reports.

TIP FROM THE **CLASSROOM**

Shake Hands Across the World

In the world outside school, collaboration often happens across distances with diverse team members connecting via online tools. Vicki Davis and Julie Lindsay, global educators who developed the Flat Classroom Project, recommend starting such projects with a "digital handshake" to build relationships among team members who may live in different regions or countries, speak different languages, or come from different cultures (Lindsay & Davis, 2012). The digital handshake might be an exchange of videos, emails, or Skype calls for students to get acquainted and start to learn about — and with — each other.

Conduct team-building activities

If students are new to collaboration, introduce them to teamwork with team-building games or mini-challenges. In Project Lion Pride, for example, teachers had teams do warm-up activities, such as coming up with team names and creating team banners. Warm-up activities should be low-stakes and even playful, such as relay races that require teamwork, puzzles that require everyone's contribution to solve, or team drawing or construction tasks such as the popular Marshmallow Challenge (**marshmallowchallenge.com**).

> Warm-up activities should be low-stakes and even playful.

After leading a warm-up activity, guide students in a debrief discussion. What helped team members work well together and bring out everyone's contributions? What got in the way of collaboration? Did everyone participate, or did just a few students take over the activity? In the discussion, help students arrive at their own definition of effective collaboration.

Another approach to foster discussion about collaboration is fishbowl modeling. Have one team of students carry out a team warm-up activity while classmates observe. For example, you could have the team plan a Superbowl party (requiring collaboration on securing a location, menu planning, seating, decorations, and so forth), or decide what movie to see that weekend (an exercise in shared decision making). Afterward, all students should be primed to discuss what they noticed about team dynamics and how collaboration might be improved in the future.

Develop norms

Have students work together to spell out class norms for the conditions that support effective teamwork. Prompt their thinking about norms by asking, "What does it look like and feel like when you are working well with each other?" Then, help them turn their observations into agreements. Encourage positives rather than negatives. For example, students might suggest, "We listen to each other without interrupting," or "We welcome and respect each other's ideas." (Those are more positive statements than, "No put-downs.") Have students capture these norms on posters or with slogans, using their own words or symbols to express how they expect team members to treat one another and contribute to shared goals. Post these norms in a visible spot in the classroom (or on your class website), and encourage students to refer back to them throughout the project.

Over time, as students become more accustomed to expectations for collaboration in PBL, they will need less help in understanding what it means.

Introduce rubrics early

If you plan to assess students on collaboration, now's the time to introduce your rubric for collaboration and make sure students know how to use it as a learning tool throughout the project. (See **Useful Stuff** for an example.) You may want to write a collaboration rubric as a whole-class activity or rewrite an existing rubric in more student-friendly language. Help students understand that the rubric offers clear guidance on what collaboration looks like in practice. It's not just a scoring guide that the teacher uses for grading, but also a useful tool to help students monitor their own progress.

If students have never been assessed on collaboration before, give them time to get familiar with the rubric. Whether you provide students with a ready-made rubric or engage them in creating it, make sure that students understand the criteria and can explain what good teamwork looks like with specific examples. You might show them a video clip of students working as a team and ask them to rate their performance, using the rubric as a scoring guide. Or you might use the fishbowl approach and have one team attempt a collaborative task. Then, observers can discuss how well students did at collaboration, using the rubric to guide their discussion. Similarly, you might have students use the rubric to assess themselves on collaboration, and then set personal goals for areas in which they want to improve.

Schools that emphasize PBL across the curriculum often use the same collaboration rubric across grades and disciplines, encouraging a common language and schoolwide culture. As you continue to emphasize the language of effective teamwork, students should internalize the message that collaboration gets better with practice.

TIP FROM THE **CLASSROOM**

Put it in Their Own Words

Here's how students in a science class described effective collaboration in their own words.

■ Top score (4 points): "I always make sure everyone gets a turn and is included. I compromise, talk respectfully and support other people's ideas."

■ Poor collaboration (earning only 1 point): "I don't help or communicate with my group members and I act like I don't want to be there." (Park & Bailey, n.d.)

Walk the talk

Reinforce a collaborative culture in your classroom by making sure all students have a voice in class discussions. For example, as soon as you launch your project with an Entry Event and Driving Question, be ready to facilitate an inclusive conversation about what students think they will need to know in order to do answer the Driving Question and complete the project. Model what it means to engage everyone in the discussion, listen respectfully, and capture questions in students' own words.

Encourage accountability

In PBL, team members are accountable to one another for meeting project goals and deadlines, balancing project responsibilities, negotiating differences, and overcoming setbacks. This is different than simply dividing up the work.

To help students understand what it means to be accountable to their fellow team members, guide them through a process for making team agreements or contracts. (See examples at **bie.org/tools**.) Contracts spell out expectations for

---

TIP FROM THE **CLASSROOM**

Use Hand Signals to Help Reach Consensus

Some PBL teachers teach students to use hand signals to indicate whether they can agree with a team decision. It could be as simple as "thumbs up, thumbs down," and "thumbs sideways" (to indicate uncertainty at this point). The "Fist to Five" method is excellent for helping students reach consensus (Rindone, 1996; Fletcher, 2002). It's useful for drawing out minority viewpoints about different positions or solutions that the team is considering and ensuring that all team members have a voice. Here's how it works:

Students use these hand signals to communicate their position:

- Fist (no fingers): It means, "No way. I need to talk more about this and need to see changes before I can support it."

- 1 finger: "Leaning toward no. I still want to discuss this and suggest changes to consider."

- 2 fingers: "So-so. I am more comfortable with the proposal but would like to discuss some minor tweaks."

- 3 fingers: "It's OK. I'm not in total agreement but can let this pass without further discussion."

- 4 fingers: "Yes. I think it's a good idea/decision.**"**

- 5 fingers: "Absolutely! This is a great idea and I will help lead its implementation."

Team members who hold up three or fewer fingers are given time to air their concerns. Discussions continue until all team members can signal their consensus for an idea by showing three or more fingers.

---

team members in student language (e.g., "No slacking"), along with a process that outlines what happens if someone lets down the team ("You're fired!"). If teams encounter turbulence during a project, encourage them to revisit their contracts instead of asking you to fix things for them. Peer pressure can exert a positive force to get unproductive team members back on track. Although students may decide to include contract language about firing team members who let down the team, such events should be rare.

Teach the art of negotiation

Differences of opinion will naturally arise during projects as students make investigations, evaluate research and different problem-solving strategies, and choose the best way to demonstrate or share what they know. Help students master the art of negotiation. Model what it means to advocate for your ideas, be open to others' suggestions, and build consensus so that everyone on the team is comfortable with team decisions. Remind students that consensus is not the same as majority rules or having the loudest voice in the room. Everyone on the team must be able to say, "I can live with this decision." Knowing how to negotiate differences of opinion will serve students well long after they leave your classroom.

Teach how to give and receive feedback

Effective collaborators are able to give and receive critical feedback that enables their team to improve its efforts. This requires artful collaboration with an emphasis on the work product rather than on the individual. PBL emphasizes cycles of revision and reflection during projects, creating multiple opportunities for students to give and receive feedback. Be deliberate about teaching students how to give and receive feedback. Ron Berger, chief program officer for Expeditionary Learning, summarizes the three rules he uses to guide peer critique: "Be kind. Be specific. Be helpful." These simple but powerful guidelines are used in a critical friends protocol everywhere from kindergarten classes to High Tech High in California, known for its high-quality student projects.

Teach students appropriate sentence stems to use when offering peer feedback, such as: I like… [be specific about what's working well] and I wonder… [be gentle with constructive criticism for improvement]. For example: In critiquing a peer's story, a student might say, "I like how you have taken time to fully develop the characters. I wonder if the reader might forget about the plot in the section where you have that really long description of…"

> Effective collaborators are able to give and receive critical feedback that enables their team to improve its efforts.

Model how to give and receive this kind of feedback, and share examples of how your own efforts have improved thanks to timely, helpful feedback from colleagues.

Look for opportunities for critical feedback — both formal and informal

Teachers at High Tech High suggest holding critiques whenever you want students to revise a draft. Here are some examples of project situations that lend themselves to critical feedback:

> Help to frame feedback by giving reviewers specific questions to consider.

- If students are blogging as part of a project, have them comment on each other's posts in a respectful way. This provides informal peer feedback throughout the project.

- Use gallery walks for more formal critique. Students display their draft products, and classmates take time to visit and respond to each exhibit. Sticky notes work well for capturing concise feedback, including suggestions for improvement and praise for elements that reviewers like. For digital projects, have students conduct their gallery walk online. Suggest specific things students should be looking for as they make the rounds.

- Use the writers' workshop model to encourage peer review in small-group settings. Help to frame feedback by giving reviewers specific questions to consider. Make sure each student has opportunities to offer and receive feedback. If students are new to the workshop approach, model it with a small group first in a fishbowl (with the rest of the class observing).

- Invite experts to offer feedback on projects while students still have time to make revisions. (Invite the same experts back for the culminating event, too.) Hint: Older students can be excellent experts for younger ones.

Use formative assessment tools

Use informal observations, reflection prompts for journaling or discussion, exit slips, and other tools to check on how well teams are working together. For example:

- **Project logs** track the status of specific tasks that teams need to accomplish by key deadlines, alerting you quickly if they are running into challenges. (See **bie.org/tools** for sample project management log).

- **Reflection questions** that focus specifically on team dynamics can elicit timely information about team challenges.

- **Have students self-assess** their collaboration abilities throughout a project. For example, students might use different colored highlighters to show where they are on a collaboration rubric at specific dates. At a glance, they can see if they are progressing toward mastery or identify areas that need improvement.

Reinforce conflict resolution strategies

Differences of opinion are inevitable if students are engaging in genuine give-and-take during projects. If tensions escalate, however, be ready to help students resolve their differences peacefully and respectfully. If formative assessment tells you that teams are having trouble getting along, be ready to step in with support or coaching to help them air out conflicts and get back on track. For example, suggest holding a team meeting or offer a mini-lesson on how to build consensus if team members disagree about the direction to go with a project. If students signed a team contract at the start of the project, use this document to frame discussions about accountability. If a team member isn't living up to his or her agreement, refer the student to the contract and be ready to help the team apply the consequences called for in the document.

TIP FROM THE **CLASSROOM**

"Go have a meeting."

This is what veteran PBL teacher Terry Smith says to help his students deal with conflicts that inevitably arise during projects. Rather than relying on the teacher to resolve issues, students learn to work through their own differences. Teach your students to hold meetings that have an agenda (What are we discussing?), process (Everyone gets a chance to speak), and outcome (What is our next step?). You may want to first model a team meeting with the whole class or in a fishbowl to introduce this approach. Sit in as observer when students start to conduct their own meetings.

Determine

Near the end of the project, as you prepare students for presenting their work to an audience, you can begin to determine how effectively students have collaborated throughout the project. As students demonstrate what they know and can do as a result of the project, be thinking about how these results were enhanced by teamwork (or limited by a lack of it).

Students shouldn't be surprised to learn that they will be graded on teamwork; your rubric made your criteria for assessment clear from the start. Nonetheless, team members may have differing opinions about who contributed what to the project.

Norms Help High-Achievers Work in Teams

A teacher named Shelley Wright found that her academically high-achieving students struggled when she introduced them to PBL in 12th-grade English. Accustomed to working individually, these college-bound seniors had not yet learned how to set goals or negotiate differences as a team, offer constructive peer feedback, or make good use of each other's talents. "I almost felt like we were starting too late," she said, but she wisely decided it was important to build students' collaboration abilities to prepare them for life after high school. "In our first project, they thought that collaborating meant dividing up the work and then never talking to each other again," Wright said.

That attitude made teamwork a challenge, so Wright prompted students to establish norms for working together. As a class, they reflected on, "What would you like to go better next time? What do you need to know about how to work together to accomplish better results?" Their discussion elicited agreements about how to share responsibilities for team products, be accountable to shared deadlines, and improve each other's ideas through respectful feedback. With norms in place, their next project not only went more smoothly, but students produced higher-quality work as a result of their improved collaboration capabilities.

To assess collaboration fairly, combine your own observations of what was happening during the project with:

- **Self-assessments:** Have students rate their own team contributions and growth as collaborators, with evidence and specifics to back up their self-assessments.

- **Peer assessments:** Have team members anonymously assess each other's contributions or shortcomings as collaborators. Again, ask for evidence and specific examples.

- **Questioning:** When students present their project, ask follow-up questions that require them to go off script. Are all members of the team able to defend their conclusions or explain how they arrived at a particular position? Ask students about their process for working as a team and any challenges they had to overcome to work together effectively. How did they share leadership responsibilities as well as workload?

TECH TIP ▸ Tools for Collaboration

A wide range of technology tools support collaborative practice. Here are a few to consider using with your students:

- **Edmodo**, mentioned previously as a site for connecting with fellow PBL teachers, also offers tools to support collaboration among your students. As a teacher, you can set up secure online communities just for your classes. Edmodo helped students stay organized throughout Project Lion Pride by giving them a shared online workspace.

- **Web-based tools** such as Google Docs enable students to work on shared documents. Because students can access their docs from any computer connected to the Internet, they can work together on projects outside of class.

- **Wikis** enable multiple authors to add to a single website, allowing students to crowdsource content. The History feature on a wiki enables teachers to track which students have added or modified content.

- **Real-time editing tools** let team members write and edit a document at once. Tools such as Titanpad.com and Sync.in display each author's text in a different color. A chat window on the same screen as the text allows for "Bulletin Board" conversations.

- **Digital publishing tools** like VoiceThread (**voicethread.com**) allow students to make comments or offer feedback using text or short voice recordings.

- **Skype**, a platform for voice-over Internet protocol (**education.skype.com**), allows students to make video calls anywhere in the world. Students can use Skype to stay connected with team members in other locations or engage with remote experts for feedback.

- **Quick Screen Share** allows collaborators to share their computer screens with a simple click (**quickscreenshare.com**).

Draw on all information sources to get a full picture of students' strengths and weak spots as collaborators.

After the project's culminating event, be sure to have students reflect on their team experience. If they faced challenges working with their team, ask them to imagine how things might go better next time. Where do they see room to improve? Have them set their own goals for how they want to get better at collaborating.

Final Thought: Be a Collaborator Yourself

Model teamwork by making collaboration part of your professional life, just as teachers did at Howe High School. Let students know that you work with colleagues to plan and improve on projects. If you use digital tools to connect with a professional learning network, help students see that collaborating connects you with good ideas from around the globe.

Here are some ideas for incorporating more collaboration into your own work:

- Invite feedback from your colleagues when you are planning projects. Be specific about feedback you are seeking. For example: Do they find your Driving Question engaging?

- Use Google Docs or other collaborative documents to create content together with colleagues.

- Take part in online discussions (such as #Edchat or #PBLchat, weekly events that happen on Twitter) to exchange ideas with colleagues from around the globe.

- Use social media sites for education to connect with colleagues who share your interest in PBL. For example, BIE hosts an active PBL community on Edmodo (**edmodo.com/biepbl**).

Collaboration Throughout a Project

with Common Core Alignment

Launching the Project

An engaging Entry Event and open-ended Driving Question launch students on their inquiry experience. Need to Know discussions raise questions that will guide students' investigation.

Building Knowledge, Understanding and Skills

Students learn necessary content knowledge from the teacher, readings, and other resources, and gain skills that will help them create project products and answer the Driving Question. They do research, test hypotheses, and gather and analyze data.

Collaboration Opportunities

▶ Students develop norms for effective teamwork.

▶ Students work together to identify "Need to Know" questions for the project.

▶ Students create and monitor a task list, team roles, and a schedule for project work. (CC ELA 6-12.SL.1b)

▶ Students agree on how to use technology tools to communicate and manage project tasks.

▶ Students work in teams to do inquiry-based research.

▶ Students prepare for and participate effectively in a range of collaborative discussions with diverse partners. (CC ELA 6-12.SL.1)

▶ Students follow rules for collegial discussions (CC ELA 6-12.SL.1b), decision-making, and conflict resolution.

Developing and Revising Ideas and Products

Students consider diverse perspectives and generate multiple solutions, designs, and answers to the Driving Question. Through cycles of critical feedback, they refine their thinking and improve on early ideas as they create final products.

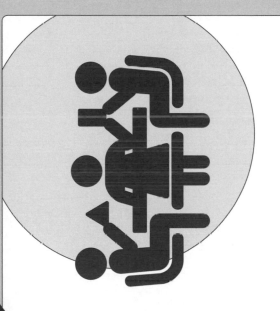

- ▶ Students understand the approaches of others for solving complex problems. (CC ELA 6-12.SL.1d)
- ▶ Students build on others' ideas and express their own clearly and persuasively. (CC ELA 6-12.SL.1)
- ▶ Students use technology to produce shared writing products. (CC ELA 6-12.W.6)
- ▶ Students give and receive critical feedback to improve written products (CC ELA 6-12.W.5) and evaluate problem solutions, product designs, and answers to the Driving Question.

Presenting Products and Answers to Driving Questions

Students share the results of their efforts with a public audience, demonstrating what they learned in the project. They explain and defend their research, product design, and strategies for problem solving. Finally, they reflect on their experience.

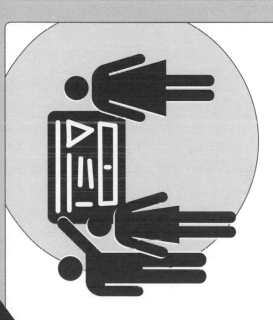

- ▶ Team members decide how best to use multimedia components, visual displays, and digital media in presentations. (CC ELA 6-12.SL.5)
- ▶ Team members share responsibility for presenting work effectively to a public audience. (CC ELA 6-12.SL.4)

61

Bulletin Board Thoughts on Communication

Communication is two-sided — vital and profound communication makes demands also on those who are to receive it... demands in the sense of concentration, of genuine effort to receive what is being communicated.

> — **Roger Sessions,**
> **American composer**

One of the most important skills to have in business is the ability to translate complex concepts into plain English.

> — **Myra Drucker,**
> **business executive**

I'm a great believer that any tool that enhances communication has profound effects in terms of how people can learn from each other, and how they can achieve the kind of freedoms that they're interested in.

> — **Bill Gates,**
> **founder of Microsoft**

Take advantage of every opportunity to practice your communication skills so that when important occasions arise, you will have the gift, the style, the sharpness, the clarity, and the emotions to affect other people.

> — **Jim Rohn,**
> **entrepreneur and author**

COMMUNICATION IN PBL

It's a sign of the times that an elite university like MIT requires students to take "communication-intensive" courses. The next generation of scientists and engineers won't succeed on technical merits alone. Aspiring experts also need to be able to explain their good ideas, both in writing and in oral presentations. To succeed in careers, they will need to be able to turn research data into publishable articles and advocate for support to further their investigations. For those heading into entrepreneurial fields, knowing how to deliver a convincing "pitch" to funders is a modern-day business survival skill. Managers and workers in many of today's workplaces may be called upon to explain procedures and share information, train others, or explain their ideas in a meeting.

In today's Information Age, everyone has access to communication tools and publishing platforms. With publishing flattened by technology, anyone can be a content creator. The downside, of course, is the potential for information overload. It takes a skilled communicator to be heard above the din. That helps explain why strong communication abilities are essential across a wide range of disciplines. Knowing how to convey ideas and connect with audiences has become a highly prized capability, not only in science and engineering but also in the arts, politics, media, and many more fields.

Beyond college and careers, students need to be able to communicate well to participate fully in society. Engaged citizens do more than vote. They exchange opinions and insights about the issues of the day. That might mean discussing local issues with neighbors, taking part in political campaigns or nonprofit activities, or advocating for solutions in their communities or on the national stage. Today's students will need a range of communication skills for their day-to-day activities, from communicating with their health care providers via phone or emails to getting across their opinions via social media to listening carefully to what their future children's teachers have to share.

Competence and Confidence as Communicators

Communication encompasses a range of competencies, many of which come into play in PBL. Most projects require students to collaborate (as we discussed in Chapter 3). For collaboration to be effective, of course, team members need to know how to share information and exchange ideas respectfully. Students often consult with experts as part of their research or when creating authentic products. Here, too, good communication is essential.

Some projects connect students with people whose cultural or language traditions are different from their own. Learning to communicate across

---

Bulletin Board | # Communication and the Common Core

Being able to communicate effectively is an expectation throughout the Common Core. In addition to ELA standards for written communication, the speaking and listening standards emphasize that students need to become adept at understanding when to speak formally, when it's OK to use more informal jargon, and how to decide the best means of presenting their ideas to an audience.

Speaking and listening standards specifically call on students to:

- Present claims and findings using relevant, well-chosen descriptions, facts, details, and examples to support main ideas and themes (CC 6-8.SL.4)

- Use relevant evidence and sound, valid reasoning (CC 8.SL.4)

- State main idea and move from one idea to the next in a focused manner, in an order that makes sense; emphasize most important points (CC 6-8. SL.4)

- Speak appropriately for the context and task, demonstrating command of formal English when appropriate (CC 6-8.SL.6)

- Use well-produced multimedia components or visual displays to help emphasize most important points, clarify information, and add interest (CC 6-7.SL.5)

- Use multimedia components or visual displays to strengthen claims and evidence (CC 8.SL.5)

Math standards similarly reinforce being able to communicate with precision:

- Mathematically proficient students try to communicate precisely to others. They try to use clear definitions in discussion with others and in their own reasoning. (CC 6-12.MP.6)

Communication: What should you see?

During a classroom visit, what should you look for if you want to know that students are building their capacity to communicate? If you are a school leader doing a classroom walk-through, instructional coach offering feedback on PBL practices, or colleague providing peer critique, look for evidence that students are being given opportunities to develop their communication capabilities. How often do you see students:

- Convey their ideas using media other than a written paper (for example, with posters, presentation software, videos, or blogs)?
- Prepare and deliver an oral presentation (to teacher, peers, or community members)?
- Answer questions in front of an audience?
- Decide how they will present their work or demonstrate their learning?
- Create tables, graphs, charts, or other products to communicate data in written or oral presentations?

These questions can be useful for reflecting on your own practice, too. Ask yourself whether you notice your students struggling with any of the activities listed above. If you have had to overcome reluctance or nervousness about public speaking, what has helped you become a more confident communicator? Are you teaching and modeling a variety of ways to communicate with your own classroom behaviors?

cultures helps students develop global awareness in our flattened world. Learning to use technology tools to communicate across distances helps students develop technical fluency. These abilities are more hallmarks of 21st century communicators.

During a project, students need to be able to organize their ideas and develop original content. They may need to choose from a variety of media to select the format best suited for sharing their work. At the end of the project, students publicly showcase what they have learned, often in oral presentations where they explain why it matters and respond to audience questions. Such culminating events put students into real-life situations similar to those that scientists, policy makers, journalists, artists, entrepreneurs, and others experience in the course of doing their work. Through repeat experiences of presenting their work to audiences, students develop both competence and confidence as skilled communicators.

To build proficiency, students need to practice communicating across a variety of media and for many authentic purposes. Projects provide the ideal context for introducing these competencies and for helping students get better at them by putting their communications toolkit to work.

Let's take a closer look at one project in which students were taught how to communicate effectively and learned the advantage of building this competency.

Project Spotlight: Be an Entrepreneur

What does it take to start your own business? Seventh graders from Middle School 223 in the Bronx have some keen insights about this question. Their in-depth investigation into entrepreneurship involved coming up with ideas for new consumer products or services, and then pitching their business plans to experts from finance, engineering, and related fields at an expo. Top-rated teams went on to compete in a regional event, facing off against other young entrepreneurs from across New York City.

Technology teacher Nicole Lentino has several goals for the annual project, which she developed in collaboration with the nonprofit Network for Teaching Entrepreneurship. She wants her students, most from low-income families, to explore careers and recognize their own potential to succeed in business. Few students have ever met a business owner before. "This is new territory for them,"

> To set the stage for teamwork, Lentino deliberately teaches behaviors like active listening.

Lentino says. That means she has to challenge stereotypes "so they can see that they can be successful in owning their own business someday. We want them to think about how planning for a career can help you take control of your future."

Launching the project

The project, which addresses Common Core standards for speaking, listening, and writing, emphasizes effective communication from start to finish. To set the stage for teamwork, Lentino deliberately teaches behaviors like active listening. She also models effective communication in the way she explains the project, identifying specific learning goals for every activity. "This helps students understand why we're doing it. I make my whole plan transparent," she says.

To help students consider a range of career options before they start to plan their businesses, Lentino brings in guest speakers from diverse fields. These experts offer students insights about working in different fields and also model how to give an effective presentation. While students are exploring careers, they also are taking stock of their own interests, strengths, and expectations. Lentino encourages students to consider, "Does the reality of a career match what you want in the future? If not, do you need to adjust what you want in terms of income or lifestyle? Or maybe consider a different field?"

Building knowledge and skills

As the project moves into the extended inquiry phase, students work in teams to come up with original ideas for consumer products or services that would serve genuine market needs in their own community. Each team is required to produce and market a single business plan. That means students need to listen closely to each other's creative suggestions and then reach consensus about which idea they want to pitch at the expo. "I knew we had to communicate, but I really learned how to talk to my team," one of the students reflected after doing the project.

> Students consider the role of various tech tools — such as blogging, social media, and apps — in business communication.

Students also test potential ideas through market research. Because Lentino wants students to consider an authentic audience, she designed the project so that students focus on the needs of their own community. They might survey classmates or community members to find out if an idea has local appeal. This is important research for developing their written business plan, and it's also good preparation for tailoring their "pitch" to appeal to their target audience.

Developing products

Writing a business plan means students need to organize their research and also apply new concepts, such as market analysis and risk assessment. They bring a businesslike approach to communication as they develop logos, business cards, and other marketing materials. Lentino integrates technology by having students consider the role of various tech tools — such as blogging, social media, and apps — in business communication. At the same time, she emphasizes face-to-face communication. "We devote a whole lesson to how to give a proper handshake," she says.

Working with diverse learners, Lentino differentiates instruction by making all project materials available on a collaborative Google site. Students who are ready to charge ahead have all the resources they need, allowing Lentino to work with smaller groups that need more instructional support to be successful.

Presenting products

As the project moves toward its culmination, the focus shifts to preparing for public presentations. Lentino breaks the ice by acknowledging that she sometimes gets nervous when speaking to groups. "I tell them I'm adult, I'm confident, but I still get nervous," she says. That allows students to own up to the jitters they may be feeling, and also sets the stage for practice sessions that will get them ready to present with confidence.

Lentino carefully scaffolds the public speaking aspect of the project. She eases students into presenting to an audience. First they talk just with their own teammates, then to another team, before gradually building up to addressing the whole class. The practice sessions emphasize both style and content as factors that will influence an audience. For example, Lentino coaches students to think on their feet as part of making a convincing pitch. "We talk about who their audience is and how they plan to persuade them. Will they overload their presentation with evidence, or allow audience members to ask questions? How will students be prepared to answer different questions? What if they don't know an answer? How should they respond?" Considering all these contingencies helps students feel better prepared to make convincing presentations.

At the business plan expo that wraps up the project, each student team presents its concept to an audience that includes peers, parents, and business experts who are there as official judges. Audience members stroll among the poster-style exhibits. Judges are recruited by the National Foundation for Teaching Entrepreneurship and are prepared in advance on how to use rubrics to assess students' presentations.

Students use props and poster-style exhibits to add interest to their presentations, along with snappy slogans and business names to make their pitches memorable. For instance, one team proposed launching a local bakery called the Charmed Bake Shoppe. When judges asked why the neighborhood needed a bakery, students were ready with detailed financial and demographic

Bulletin Board

Research Snapshot:
PBL Teachers Scaffold Communication

Interacting with an authentic audience, a key to successful PBL, sets a high bar for students. Students are motivated to do their best work when they know it's time for the spotlight, but they need frequent practice and feedback to get good at answering unexpected questions and fine-tuning their presentations to appeal to their audience. Some 83% of teachers who emphasize PBL create opportunities for students to engage with audiences at least monthly; only 50% of teachers who do not use PBL create monthly audience interactions for students. PBL students are also more likely to make decisions about the best way to convey their ideas in presentations. This happens at least monthly for 79% of students in PBL settings, but only 32% of students in non-PBL classes have the same experience.

Source: Hixson, Ravitz, and Whisman, 2012

information about the market gap they sought to fill. One judge challenged them on investing in a bricks-and-mortar store rather than a mobile bakery van. Again, students were ready with an answer: Their proposed shop would feature free wi-fi so that students could do their homework there. Unlike a mobile van, a shop would create a community gathering spot for people of all ages.

At the end of the high-energy pitch sessions, judges praised students' grace under pressure. "We asked questions and they responded seamlessly," one businessperson told a visiting reporter.

Watching her diverse students make their presentations with confidence has convinced Lentino of the value of this extended project. One special-needs student, for example, arrived for the business expo formally dressed. "He spoke to adults clearly, calmly, and was happy doing it," she recalls. In students' reflections after the expo, Lentino can hear a shift in attitude. "They see now how they can be successful in business." And, they understand the critical role of communication to achieve their goals.

Your Turn: Design, Develop, and Determine

To teach and assess communication in PBL, use a three-part approach:

Design

It's impossible to imagine a project that does not involve several forms of communication. Sharing project results with a public audience is one of the essential elements of high-quality PBL, and for good reason. Experience shows that providing students with an authentic audience makes projects more meaningful and engaging than simply turning in assignments to a teacher. Long before students arrive at their final presentations, however, they will be need to communicate with peers and experts, organize their ideas, consider their audience, and select which of various modes will be best suited for showcasing their work. Good communication is essential across the arc of the project, not just on presentation day. As you design the project, consider opportunities in which students will communicate in an authentic manner or real-world context. In the entrepreneurship project, for instance, students shared their projects with judges at pitch sessions, just as entrepreneurs do when looking for backers. If the project involves historical research, you might have students display their work in the style of an interactive museum exhibit. If students are addressing a local challenge or issue, they could share their findings with interested policymakers, a local government agency, or the people most likely to benefit from their proposed solutions. In each case, students

> Consider opportunities in which students will communicate in an authentic manner or real-world context.

would need to consider how to construct their message to communicate with their intended audience.

At the project planning stage, decide which elements of the project to formally assess. Grading students on their presentations is common practice in PBL, given the emphasis on sharing or demonstrating work with a public audience. However, you may decide to emphasize a different 21st century competency in a particular project, and your scoring plan will reflect that. Even if you don't assign points for presentation skills, however, you still will want to encourage effective communication at all stages of the project.

Be ready to share your assessment plan with students so that they can anticipate what "successful communication" will look like in the project. As you plan your project calendar, consider how you will use formative assessment throughout the project, too, to check on and support students' developing communication abilities.

> Share your assessment plan with students so that they can anticipate what "successful communication" will look like in the project.

Remember, encouraging good communication doesn't mean the project will take longer to do. In fact, as students get better at organizing and expressing their ideas and better communicating with teammates, don't be surprised if their project work gets more efficient.

Develop

Your students are already experienced communicators. After all, they have been practicing and honing their listening and speaking skills since infancy. By middle school and high school, they are also likely to be heavy consumers of media messages, especially those targeted to youth audiences. If they use social media sites like Facebook or content sharing sites like YouTube, they may be experienced content creators, as well. Help students see that they can build on all these experiences to become more effective communicators and more aware of how they are affected by being on the receiving end of messages.

To develop students' communication capabilities throughout a project, anticipate key issues and be ready with additional supports, as needed. Use the following guidelines to help you build students' understanding of what good communication is, create a classroom culture that supports it, and provide scaffolding for more effective communication.

Set the stage

To set the stage for projects that will involve "live" presentations, help students understand why learning to communicate well is important for college and career readiness. For example, you could have recent alumni from your school report back from college about how they have had to use various communication skills to be successful. Or you might invite guests (including parents) to talk about the importance of making presentations in their work. Ask students to share examples of people they admire — from celebrities to reality show contestants to politicians — who are able to connect with audiences. Show examples of recorded events, such as TED Talks (**ted.com**) or speeches from the Oval Office, and have students critique them. Ask students to identify what makes these messages or performances memorable (for better or worse).

Clarify what it looks like

Once you have established the importance of effective communication as a life skill, get more specific by engaging students in defining what makes for a good presentation in PBL. Have students look at examples (either live demonstrations or videos found on YouTube or archived from previous projects), and critique them together. Share examples across a wide range — from stellar to poor — and help students think critically about what makes them so.

Help students further understand what effective communication looks like by introducing the rubric you will use for assessing this competency. You might want to use or adapt the sample we provide in **Useful Stuff,** use a common rubric if your school has one, or write one with your students. Be sure that students can explain the rubric, using their own vocabulary. Have students work together to create a list of qualities that describe a good presentation. Incorporate their student-friendly language into your assessment plan, and refer back to the plan throughout the project. When you hear or see students communicating their ideas clearly and convincingly, point it out. Encourage students to do the same — whether they're praising a fellow student's clear communication style or reflecting on their own success as communicators.

Backfill as needed

Early in the project, consider your students' current abilities as communicators. What have they learned from previous projects that will help them in this one? Do they have much prior experience speaking in public, engaging with experts, or developing multimedia presentations? Do they express any anxiety or nervousness about speaking before an audience?

Create low-risk opportunities for all students to practice communicating with a purpose.

Be prepared to backfill communication competencies that students have not yet developed or in which they are weak by incorporating the scaffolds described below. Take into account the needs of diverse learners, too. Create low-risk opportunities for all students to practice communicating with a purpose. Small-group or paired activities lower the stress level when it comes to speaking in front of others. English learners and students who tend

Bulletin Board — Café Conversations

Café-style conversations encourage active participation in small-group discussions. As participants take part in rounds of conversations with different people, they start to notice patterns and make connections between ideas.

When: Use café conversations throughout a project to focus small-group discussions on development of key ideas. For example, use café discussions to help students make better sense of shared reading or to encourage diverse perspectives about possible project solutions.

How: The World Café, a nonprofit that facilitates collaborative conversations globally, has developed a discussion format that can be adapted to the classroom. Keys to the process include:

Friendly setting: Students gather in table groups of four. The World Café encourages a welcoming, café-style setting by putting butcher paper and pens on the tables to encourage purposeful doodling and note-taking. Have more proficient English learners sit with less proficient EL students. The higher-level students can model academic conversations and provide less-proficient EL students with helpful feedback.

Inviting question: An opening question frames the conversation (much as in Socratic questioning, described in Chapter 2, page 32).

Small-group rounds: Participants discuss the question for 10 to 20 minutes, and then each student from a table moves to a different table. They leave behind table notes to provide a history of their conversation for the next group that gathers there.

Debrief: After the small-group discussions, students share insights or other results from their conversations with the rest of the large group.

to be quiet in class may need additional support, encouragement, and practice to build their confidence and find their voice. (See Bulletin Board on page 79: Helping English Learners Meet 21st Century Communication Goals.)

Based on what you know about your students' current strengths and weaknesses, plan for just-in-time instruction and scaffolding throughout the project to introduce or reinforce specific communication capabilities.

Emphasize active speaking *and* listening

Knowing how to listen respectfully to fellow team members is an essential capability in PBL. It's part of collaboration (which we discussed in detail in Chapter 3), but important enough to emphasize again when you're focusing on communication. If your students are new to PBL, plan to deliberately teach and reinforce respectful listening skills so that all team members have a chance to express their ideas.

Comedian Fran Leibowitz famously observed, "The opposite of talking is not listening. The opposite of talking is waiting." That may be good for a laugh, but genuine communication involves both sending and receiving information. Help students improve at communication by emphasizing what researchers call *active listening* and *active speaking* (Marzano & Heflebower, 2012).

An active listener pays attention and provides feedback that helps the speaker articulate his or her thoughts more clearly. Model and deliberately teach active listening.

> A simple routine like think-pair-share reinforces good communication.

For example, a simple routine like think-pair-share reinforces good communication. It gives students a moment to gather their thoughts about a question ("think"), then express their idea to a peer ("pair"), before sharing their ideas — or their partner's, if you choose — with the larger group ("share"). Visible Thinking, a project of Harvard's Project Zero, recommends using this routine to promote understanding through active reasoning and explanation. Although think-pair-share seems straightforward, you may need to model the routine for students to learn to take turns, listen carefully, and ask each other questions to make sure they understand (and can sum up) the other person's statement. If students are new to using this routine, introduce and reinforce these processes and provide visual cues to help them remember the three steps.

To reinforce a culture of active listening, encourage students to show respect for a speaker, even if they disagree. For example, teach them how to use sentence starters to frame counterarguments, such as, "I see your point, but have you thought about..." Teach listeners to ask clarifying questions to make sure they understand the speaker's point of view. They might paraphrase what they've heard or start a question by saying, "Just to make sure I understand what you're saying...." Remind students that their body language (such as eye contact, head nodding, or note-taking) provides important feedback to the speaker. Once again, fishbowl-style demonstrations and teacher modeling will give students opportunities to see and internalize these behaviors.

On the other side of the conversation, active speaking involves deliberate use of words, gestures, and tone of voice to connect with listeners. Encourage active speaking by reminding students to summarize their key points and ask questions to check on listeners' understanding. Be sure students understand that developing these habits while working with their small teams will better prepare them for when it's time to speak to larger audiences.

If these habits are new to your students, use reminders (such as student-made posters or graphics) to make effective team communication part of your classroom culture.

Communicate with outside experts

PBL sets the stage for students to go outside the classroom and learn from experts. As part of their entrepreneurship project, for instance, Lentino's students conducted research in their community to learn from local business owners about the rewards and challenges of starting a small business. Make the most of these learning opportunities by preparing students for interviews with experts. By investing in preparation, students will come away with better information, and experts will know that their time has been well spent.

To help students communicate more effectively with experts:

- Teach a mini-lesson about how to prepare interview questions. Go back to the Need to Know list that you made with students when you launched the project. How might experts help students answer these questions? What else might experts know that could be useful? Is there research that would be useful to do before the interview?

- Remind students to document their interviews. Do they plan to record the interview? What equipment might they need? Perhaps one team member will

---

TIP FROM THE **CLASSROOM**

Remind Students of Norms

A teacher named Jill Thompson places these reminder cards on tables when teams are working together:

- **Encourage**: Ask questions of others.

- **Listen**: Use eye contact, respond to comments, and ask questions to show you are listening.

- **Allow for different perspectives**: Be flexible and open-minded.

- **Take turns**: Don't dominate.

ask questions and another will take notes. Have them make these assignments in advance so they don't waste time during the interview.

- Have students do role-plays with their peers to practice interviewing skills before they sit down with experts. Coach them to them to ask open-ended questions and help them plan follow-up questions. Pair English learners with fluent English speakers for these practice sessions so that EL students gain more opportunities to practice speaking and listening.

- Teach students to use technology to expand their access to experts. Using email or Skype, they can tap expertise from anywhere in the world. Open doors for students by reaching out to your professional network — or ask parents to help — to find willing experts or mentors for student projects. For Project Lion Pride (described in Chapter 3), teacher Tammy Parks found online mentors for her students by tweeting out a request for volunteers via her Twitter network.

Build toward presentations

Presenting to a public audience is a hallmark of PBL. This is when students demonstrate what they know or can do as a result of their in-depth inquiry, often using visuals or multimedia to make their case. Having an authentic audience makes projects more meaningful to students, but also means they will feel the pressure to perform well publicly. Help students think critically about what makes for a good presentation. Create or share a presentation rubric with students, such as the one found in **Useful Stuff**. As a whole-class activity, critique videos of previous culminating events. Look at examples from outside the classroom, too. One teacher has his students critique TED Talks (**ted.com**), which feature high-profile thinkers discussing a wide range of topics. Students look for tips and tricks they can borrow from the pros to improve their own presentations.

> Help students think critically about what makes for a good presentation.

As part of project scaffolding, build in time and instruction to help students prepare and organize their content, and also practice presenting before an audience. Here are some guidelines:

- **Teach Speaking Skills.** Most students will need to improve their ability to speak well when delivering a presentation. Talk about the techniques used by effective speakers, offer tips, model correct behaviors, and plan practice sessions that will help students*:
  - ▶ appear calm and confident
  - ▶ make their voice heard by all
  - ▶ put passion into their voice

▸ use eye contact to engage listeners

▸ use gestures that match their words

▸ pace their speaking for a more powerful effect

*Adapted from *Well Spoken* by Erik Palmer. See this book and other resources in the Appendix for ideas on how to conduct lessons in public speaking.

■ **Plan for Effective Presentations.** Help students plan effective presentations by considering their audience, content, organization, and visual components they have to share. See the Presentation Plan at **bie. org/tools** as an example of a tool to help students organize their ideas and materials.

Multimedia elements can add interest to presentations, but poorly executed visuals can detract from the overall message. Help students think critically about using visual or multimedia elements in their presentations. Whether they are producing a three-fold poster board, slideshow, video, or project website, they need to focus on the key information they want to impart. To help students design better media for their presentations:

▸ Communicate your expectations with a scoring guide or rubric that defines quality presentations

▸ Schedule class time with a school media specialist, art or technology teacher, or outside experts who can help students plan and produce effective presentations

▸ Share samples of visuals from previous projects and have students critique them (using a rubric or scoring guide)

■ **Practice, Practice, Practice!** Incorporate time in your project calendar for students to practice their presentations and act as audience members for other teams. Teach students how to be good audience members, too! Prompt peer reviewers to make keen observations by giving them a handout to guide their listening and capture their notes. Ask them to watch, listen for, and make notes about specific points, such as:

Give students a reality check before the big event by videotaping them in a dress rehearsal.

▸ Did the speaker's body language/eye contact/tone of voice help to hold your attention?

▸ Were visual aids useful for helping you understand key ideas or distracting from the message?

▸ How would you improve this presentation?

▸ Was anything unclear or confusing?

Give students a reality check before the big event by videotaping them in a dress rehearsal. Have students critique their own performance, using the same scoring guide that audience members will be given, if you plan to give them one. Are they dressed appropriately for a formal event? Do they think their body language and voice will engage their audience? Do they convey enthusiasm for the ideas they want to communicate?

Build Toward Larger Audiences

At schools in the High Tech High network, public exhibitions of student work are part of the culture. Each project ends with a well-attended showcase event. Getting students comfortable speaking in front of big audiences takes time, acknowledges ninth-grade Humanities teacher Diana Cornejo-Sanchez. With her incoming freshman, she eases them into giving presentations. Students present at first in front of just a few peers. As a next step, they present to their whole class. After that, they might present to a different class. With each audience, students receive helpful feedback to improve their presentations (practicing the critique skills described in Chapter 2). By the end of their freshman year, her students are comfortable sharing their work in front of audiences that number in the hundreds.

Provide just-in-time support for presentations

Spend time observing student teams as they prepare for presentations. If you see students struggling or expressing a lack of confidence about their presentations, be ready with just-in-time help or redirection.

If public presentations are new to your students, build their confidence by planning low-risk practice sessions where they work in pairs or small groups. This strategy can be helpful for students who are reluctant to speak up in front of groups, including some English learners.

If students are struggling to get across key points, teach them to succinctly convey their ideas by making an "elevator pitch." Short by design (the length of an elevator ride!), the elevator pitch forces students to get to the point quickly. While they are still at the stage when they have time to revise their presentations, encourage them to make short pitches that describe their ideas or research findings in a few pithy sentences. This gives you a quick look at how their presentations are developing.

Pair Bilingual Students with ELs

If you have bilingual students, pair them with your English learners for practice sessions, suggests Maria Alzugaray, coordinator of the bilingual program in San Jose (CA) Unified School District. "Your bilingual students are gold! They can be language brokers." She encourages peers to give each other gentle feedback about English pronunciation as well as the content of their presentations. "Model how to give feedback by asking, 'Do you mean...?' Or, 'Try saying it this way.'" (See more tips for EL students in the Bulletin Board, page 79.)

If students have the jitters, use reflection prompts to find out more about how they're feeling. Are they looking forward to the event? Do they feel prepared and confident? If their reflections instead reveal anxiety about upcoming presentations, that's a clue to offer just-in-time tips, schedule extra practice, or share advice to overcome stage fright.

If team dynamics are a concern, find out more through reflection prompts or questioning. Are all team members getting a voice in the final presentation or is someone on the team dominating? If there are concerns about a weak performer, remind team members how to be a critical friend. Are team members communicating with each other regularly about their progress? (A reflection prompt might ask: "Are you all in the loop?") If a team is encountering challenges, help guide discussions toward solutions rather than placing blame. If your assessment plan calls for grading team presentations, remind students that successful presentations involve all members of the team.

If you or your students want to practice before live audiences, start by having them give their presentations to students who are younger than they are. This gives the presenters a low-stakes opportunity to test-drive their presentations, using clear, accessible language. As a bonus, it puts younger students in the role of providing helpful focus group feedback (giving them practice with authentic communication, too).

If students need more specific feedback to improve their presentations, review the handouts (described earlier) that ask them to take notes about key aspects of the practice session. Draw out more details to make feedback more helpful. For example: How did the speaker emphasize key points? Which visuals were most helpful? How did the speaker engage you personally?

Helping English Learners Meet 21st Century Communication Goals in PBL

Communication in PBL is important for all students, but especially so for English learners. With the right scaffolding, projects offer these students—who represent the fastest-growing demographic in U.S. classrooms—an ideal context to improve communication across all four domains of reading, writing, speaking, and listening.

How can you support the success of EL students so that will they develop 21st century competencies along with language fluency?

"**Start by knowing who your EL students are** and knowing their language proficiency," advises Rosanna Mucetti, BIE's director of district and state initiatives. As both teacher and administrator, she has worked extensively with culturally and linguistically diverse student populations.

The next step is to think carefully about the language functions called for in specific 21st century learning activities, Mucetti recommends. For instance, students might be expected to communicate with a content expert or conduct a survey as part of their project research, or provide peers with critical feedback to improve work products. Teachers need to think about both "language objectives and content objectives" involved in the project, Mucetti says. "What's the language needed to engage with each task? What language would students need to participate fully? And then, how can you scaffold that with language supports so that they can be successful?"

Help EL students build specific language skills before starting a project. One widely used method follows this four-part pattern: (1) I do (direct instruction; you watch); (2) We do together (I help and respond with guided practice, questioning, instructional conversation); (3) You do together (collaborative practice among students while I watch and respond); (4) You do independently (I watch and respond).

To build EL students' confidence as communicators, provide them with models and scaffolds such as sentence starters, word walls, and graphic organizers. Make these supports visible in the classroom or provide them as handouts to EL students. For example, teach students to use a language frame such as, "If ____ happens, then _____," to show cause and effect. Help them recognize key words that signal concepts like change over time or compare and contrast. Encourage them to speak up if they disagree with a classmate by saying, "Have you thought about_____?" You're likely to find that EL students aren't the only ones who will benefit from these diplomatic reminders.

Small-group work typically means more time to practice speaking and listening with peers. To make the most of these opportunities, be deliberate about scaffolding communication skills. For example, EL students often benefit from having more time to think about their responses in a small-group setting—after all, they need time to both process their thoughts and translate them into English. Introducing a protocol like think-pair-share or teaching students to use mindmapping to make their ideas visible will better prepare EL students to take a more active part in discussions.

Scaffolds and deliberate instruction for the language a project demands will likely help all students, Mucetti adds, "but it's do or die for EL students. If they don't get the intentional, targeted language instruction at school in the project, they may not have the opportunity to access the social and academic English anywhere else."

Classroom Close-up:
Meet a PBL-EL Teacher

Amy Carrington teaches English and Spanish at Tuttle Middle School in Indiana. Her students include both native Spanish speakers and native English speakers. That means everyone's a language learner. "PBL is an excellent tool," she says. "Through projects, students explore language in depth, building from what they know."

She models what it means to be a good listener by paying close attention to students' questions and concerns, and then developing projects based on issues that offer a high degree of student interest.

One memorable project began when some students heard a rumor that the local library was going to get rid of its Spanish-language books because no one was checking them out. Once students confirmed the rumor, Carrington asked them why they thought the books were getting such little use. That question launched them on an investigation — and eventually, led to community change.

First, students discovered that the library database was in English, and thus, hard to access for those without English fluency. They also noticed that Spanish-language books were distributed around the library, making the books hard for patrons to find.

"Students decided to fix that," Carrington said. Their next step: surveying Hispanic community members about library usage. This involved thinking about the right questions to ask and how to phrase them (creating more opportunities to use communication skills for an authentic purpose). Students asked questions such as: Do you use the library? If not, why not? Are you aware of the book selection available at the library? What would you like to see when it comes to library services?

As a problem-solving strategy, students developed a Spanish-English database of the collection and presented it to the library board of directors. "They explained their research and why they had created this bilingual database. They implored the library board to consolidate all the Spanish language books in one place to make them easier to access," Carrington said. The board agreed.

As a final chapter in their project, students hosted a community celebration at the library and conducted tours of the new Spanish-language section.

"Give student avenues to do projects like this," Carrington says, "and they will grab on. It's exciting for them. The result is empowered learners."

Help EL Students Access the Project

Larry Ferlazzo and Katie Hull Sypnieski, co-authors of *The ESL/ELL Teacher's Survival Guide*, suggest investing time to learn about students' prior experiences and backgrounds so that you can better connect them to new learning. This naturally fits with PBL practices that emphasize student voice and choice, while at the same time giving EL students authentic reasons to speak and listen.

To launch a project, Ferlazzo and Sypnieski suggest using visuals such as video clips, cartoons, or photos as part of your Entry Event (rather than text heavy reading materials). After sharing a visual that relates to school bullying, for example, you might ask students to describe what they notice and discuss if they or people they know have ever encountered similar situations. Students might do role-plays or short presentations to communicate their personal connections to the issue before moving into teamwork related to potential solutions.

PBL also creates opportunities for EL students to teach others, which helps to develop their language and leadership skills, Ferlazzo and Sypnieski note. Using strategies such as jigsaws, students can become experts in one aspect of a project and then teach their classmates what they have learned. This builds their communication skills (and confidence) as well as content knowledge.

Determine

At the final stage of the project, students are in the spotlight as they communicate their understanding to an audience. For some projects, there may not be "live" presentations at the end; students may, for example, post their writing or photo essays on the web, and invite comments from readers/viewers. In either case, your role at this stage is less visible but still critically important as you manage the learning that continues during and after students present their work. How will you determine that students have met goals for effective communication?

Along with coordinating the logistics of event planning or online showcasing, you will want to think about these factors:

- Audience was something you considered back at the design stage of the project. Now is the time to review your original plan and invite more people if you or your students wish, if possible. Are there audience members you hadn't considered earlier, such as content experts that students connected with? How about people personally affected by a problem that students have attempted to solve? Beyond family and friends, who else might have a keen interest in what students have learned or produced?

- How can you facilitate audience participation so that students receive useful, authentic feedback? For example, you might want to provide audience members with feedback forms or scorecards that direct their attention to specific topics. (Was the content useful/informative/original? Was the presentation well-organized? Were the visual elements helpful for communicating the message?) Encourage audience members to ask follow-up questions that challenge students to think on their feet.

- How ready are your students for audience interactions? If this is one of their first projects (and first public presentations), you might want to start with a scenario in which audience members or judges circulate and talk one-on-one with students about their projects. Such experiences are authentic (think of gallery openings or scientific poster sessions), and put students into situations where they have to explain their work. Once they are successful in lower-key interactions, they will have more confidence for future events before bigger crowds.

The culminating event is also when you put your summative assessment plan to work. In the rubric you shared with students (or created with them) at the start of the project, you clearly explained the role that communication plays in project assessment. For example, it's likely that you set an expectation for all team members to take an active part in final presentations. If you plan to include audience scores in final assessment, let students know in advance. Share with them the scoring sheets (or online survey prompts) that you provide for audience members.

Close with Reflection

Reflection plays an important role in helping students develop as communicators. After the presentations, be sure to plan final reflection activities that prompt students to think about the role that effective communication played in the project. For example, you might ask them to reflect on what they learned from engaging with experts, or whether they would prepare for this experience differently next time. How might they improve communications with teammates on a future project? What did they learn from interacting with an audience? Were they able to connect with audience members or convince them of the value of their ideas? Did they encounter questions from the audience that they were unprepared to answer? What are their goals for continuing to develop and improve as communicators? See more reflection suggestions in **Useful Stuff**.

TECHTIP Use Technology Tools to Communicate

A wide range of technologies support students as communicators. The challenge may be in deciding which ones to integrate into a project plan. Take into consideration the key goals that students need to accomplish when it comes to communicating, and then look for tools that enable them to meet these goals. Here are just a few examples to consider at different stages of projects:

If students need to interview experts during the research phase, set up a video conference. Tools like Skype in the Classroom (**education.skype.com**) or Google Hangouts allow for free video chats with multiple parties.

To help students convey their ideas with team members as part of team communications, teach them to use a tool like Pinterest (**pinterest.com**) to create a virtual bulletin board where they can post images, sketches, and other information they want to share. Or try Padlet (**padlet.com**), formerly called Wallwisher, and have students post virtual sticky notes to communicate their ideas. Tools like these work well to encourage quieter students to contribute their ideas to the conversation.

If students want to present their work with multimedia visual aids, they can choose from tried-and-true PowerPoint or try alternatives such as Prezi (**prezi.com**). Have students create presentations using a collaborative platform like Google Docs, and they can work on them from any computer connected to the Internet.

If students want to publish their work, they can choose from a wide range of self-publishing platforms, including class websites or blogs. They might want to share their work on a student publishing site, such as Youth Voices (**youthvoices.net**) or My Hero (**myhero.com**). Some projects culminate with self-published books (or e-books). You can use a print-on-demand service like Lulu (**lulu.com**) and even sell the final product via Amazon.com and other online outlets.

Communication Throughout a Project

with Common Core Alignment

Communication Opportunities

▶ Students engage in discussions about the Driving Question and Need to Knows, practicing active listening and active speaking.

▶ Students clarify the meaning of unknown and multiple-meaning words and phrases, to gain understanding of the Driving Question and project tasks. (CC ELA 6-12.L.4)

▶ Students use formal English to interact with experts and other adults outside the classroom. (CC ELA 6-12.SL.6)

▶ Students acquire and use accurately a range of general academic and domain-specific words and phrases, and demonstrate independence in gathering vocabulary knowledge. (CC ELA 6-12.L.6)

▶ Students evaluate a speaker's point of view, reasoning, and use of evidence and rhetoric. (CC ELA 9-12.SL.3)

Launching the Project

An engaging Entry Event and open-ended Driving Question launch students on their inquiry experience. Need to Know discussions raise questions that will guide students' investigation.

Building Knowledge, Understanding and Skills

Students learn necessary content knowledge from the teacher, readings, and other resources, and gain skills that will help them create project products and answer the Driving Question. They do research, test hypotheses, and gather and analyze data.

Developing and Revising Ideas and Products

Students consider diverse perspectives and generate multiple solutions, designs, and answers to the Driving Question. Through cycles of critical feedback, they refine their thinking and improve on early ideas as they create final products.

- ▲ Students build on others' ideas and express their own clearly and persuasively. (CC ELA 6-12.SL.1)
- ▲ Students give and receive critical peer feedback, which helps them improve their products through iterative cycles of revision. (CC ELA 6-12.W.5)
- ▲ Students produce clear and coherent writing appropriate to task, purpose, and audience. (CC ELA 6-12.W.4)

Presenting Products and Answers to Driving Questions

Students share the results of their efforts with a public audience, demonstrating what they learned in the project. They explain and defend their research, product design, and strategies for problem solving. Finally, they reflect on their experience.

- ▲ Students use technology, including the Internet, to produce and publish writing. (CC ELA 6-12.W.6)
- ▲ Students present their ideas to a public audience and answer questions. (CC ELA 6-12.SL.4)
- ▲ Students make strategic use of multimedia, visual displays, and digital media in presentations. (CC ELA 6-12.SL.5)

Bulletin Board — Thoughts on Creativity

Building capacity to create and innovate in our students is central to guaranteeing the nation's competitiveness.

— President's Committee on the Arts and the Humanities

Risk is essential to creativity.

— Robert Sternberg, psychologist

The primary purpose of teaching can now shift away from 'stand and deliver' and becomes this: to be relentless about making sure every student graduates ready to tinker, create, and take initiative.

—Jennifer Medbery, founder and CEO of Kickboard

Innovation is how we will win the future.

—President Barack Obama

CREATIVITY AND INNOVATION IN PBL

Projects that provide opportunities for students to innovate and think creatively offer long-term value for learners — and, potentially, for society. According to a wide range of economists, government officials, and industry leaders, our nation's success across many sectors depends on a pipeline of good thinkers who can address tomorrow's problems with fresh ideas. A recent poll of 1,500 CEOs from 60 nations identified creativity as the top leadership competency of the future (IBM, 2010). If students are going to rise to the challenge, they need experiences with projects that teach them to solve problems and generate ideas in the way that innovators and creative thinkers do outside the classroom.

From Ideas to Action

Creativity and innovation are so closely linked that the terms are often used interchangeably. Goals for 21st century learners, such as the Framework for 21st Century Skills and the ISTE National Educational Technology Standards for Students, tend to combine them into a single category. But such lumping may not be helpful to the classroom teacher. There are subtle differences worth exploring if we want to build students' capacities in both areas.

Creativity may be easiest to spot in the arts where painters, musicians, filmmakers, dancers, and others draw on their imagination and craftsmanship to produce or perform original works. In the arts, creativity is an outlet for personal expression and a reflection of (or response to) culture. Yet the creative impulse extends far beyond the arts. Whether it's a chef dreaming up culinary delights, garage inventor devising a new gadget, or fashion lover designing affordable couture, we can find creativity emerging in virtually any setting. Even an employee at a department store who figures out a better way to serve customers or a factory worker whose suggestion improves efficiency or product quality is being creative. It's a defining aspect of being human. People who can generate and apply creative ideas have an edge in all walks of "regular" life, too. From the homeowner

Creativity and the Common Core

In broad strokes, the Common Core State Standards reinforce processes that support creative problem solving and underscore a respect for divergent thinking. In describing students who are college and career-ready, the standards for **English Language Arts** begin with the premise that students who are well-prepared for the future "appreciate that the twenty-first-century classroom and workplace are settings in which people from often widely divergent cultures and who represent diverse experiences and perspectives must learn and work together."

Speaking and listening standards set an expectation that, by 12th grade, students are engaging in conversations that "promote divergent and creative perspectives." (CC 6-12.SL.1c)

Reading standards reinforce the importance of the imagination, offering this description by way of introduction:

▶ Through reading great classic and contemporary works of literature representative of a variety of periods, cultures, and worldviews, students can vicariously inhabit worlds and have experiences much different than their own. (p. 7)

Writing standards, too, call on students to engage their imaginations. Anchor standard 3 states that students should be able to:

▶ Write narratives to develop real or imagined experiences or events using effective technique, well-chosen details, and well-structured event sequences. (CC 6-12.W.3)

By the end of high school, students should have developed a toolkit of strategies for creative narration, so that they can:

▶ Use precise words and phrases, telling details, and sensory language to convey a vivid picture of the experiences, events, setting, and/or characters. (CC 11-12.W.3d)

The process of improving work through iterative cycles of review and revision — central to the work of innovation — is reinforced in writing standards that call on students to:

▶ Develop and strengthen writing as needed by planning, revising, editing, rewriting, or trying a new approach. (CC 6-12.W.5)

▶ With some guidance and support from peers and adults, develop and strengthen writing as needed by planning, revising, editing, rewriting, or trying a new approach, focusing on how well purpose and audience have been addressed. (CC 6-8.W.5)

Math standards reinforce habits of mind that are common to innovators. Standards for Mathematical Practice call on students to:

▶ Make sense of problems and persevere in solving them. Mathematically proficient students start by explaining to themselves the meaning of a problem and looking for entry points to its solution. (CC 6-12.MP.1)

▶ Model with mathematics. Mathematically proficient students can apply the mathematics they know to solve problems arising in everyday life, society, and the workplace. (CC 6-12.MP.4)

with a penchant for do-it-yourself projects to the small business owner devising new ways to connect with customers, it pays to be creative.

Creative thinkers exhibit qualities such as emotional expressiveness, richness of imagery, flexibility, humor, and originality, according to the Torrance Tests of Creative Thinking. Cognitive abilities, personality traits, and past experiences all play a role in shaping our creative potential, but creativity is not a fixed quality; the right classroom strategies can help students discover, develop, and express their creativity (Treffinger, Young, Selby, & Shepardson, 2002). When students are engaged in creative work, they are applying the highest-order thinking skills.

Compared with creativity, innovation has a more practical feel. It's about putting good ideas into action to achieve desired change. Often, one breakthrough idea becomes the launching pad for future innovations. By introducing the first affordable automobile, for example, Henry Ford changed people's transportation habits. Decades later, innovators are still coming up with ideas to make car travel safer (seatbelts, car seats, airbags, GPS, and other enhancements), more entertaining (sound and video systems), and more environmentally sound (hybrid engines, cleaner fuels, and so forth). Similarly, Apple brought computing power to the masses — and unleashed a wave of software innovation — when it introduced the first personal computer. More recently, the advent of smart phones has set off another wave of app development. Consumers are devising their own new uses for technologies through what experts call "end-user innovation." Around the world, mobile devices are being used for everything from health education to improving financial services for the poor. In today's networked world, innovative ideas are emerging from all corners of the globe.

> Ensure that students learn to use a process for generating ideas, making improvements, and communicating their thinking to others.

There's no surefire way to predict whether your students will grow up to be tomorrow's creative thinkers or innovators, let alone whether their original ideas might one day benefit the world. But you can create opportunities for creativity to emerge in projects, such as integrating the arts to create aesthetically pleasing, clever, or original products; asking students to find fresh solutions to problems in their community; or challenging them to share their work in an unusual or original way. You also can ensure that students learn to use a process for generating ideas, making improvements, and communicating their thinking to others. Project Based Learning offers an ideal context for putting this process to work.

When students display creativity and innovation in PBL, they are able to generate and refine solutions to complex problems or tasks. This may involve investigating problems from multiple perspectives, generating original solutions

Creativity: What should you see?

During a classroom visit, what should you look for if you want to know that students are building their capacity to innovate and think creatively? If you are a school leader doing a classroom walk-through, instructional coach offering feedback on PBL practices, or colleague providing peer critique, look for evidence that students are being given opportunities to learn how to think creatively. How often do you see students:

- Use idea creation techniques such as brainstorming or concept mapping?

- Generate their own ideas about how to confront a problem or question?

- Test out different ideas and work to improve them?

- Invent a solution to a complex, open-ended question or problem?

- Create an original product or performance to express their ideas?

These questions can be useful for reflecting on your own practice, too. Ask yourself whether you see your students struggling with any of the activities listed above. Listen to student discussions. Do they stick with "safe" answers rather than offering divergent ideas? How might you make it safer for students to suggest novel or unexpected answers? Do all students have a voice when it comes to offering ideas, or do a few dominate discussions? How might you role-model the kinds of behaviors you want to encourage in your students?

or collaborating to build on others' ideas, and using iterative cycles of revision to improve solutions or products. Students present what they have learned in a manner that gets others interested and eager to support their ideas.

Project Spotlight: Solar Oven Design

Leah Penniman, a teacher at Tech Valley High School in Rensselaer, New York, looks for opportunities for her students to apply their understanding of science and math by tackling real-world challenges. Equally important is the charge for students to think creatively within the constraints of a project. "Of course you have to innovate if you're going to solve a problem," she explains, "especially if no one has solved it before."

One project challenged ninth graders to develop new designs for solar ovens and construct prototypes using simple, low-cost materials. This wasn't a simulation. Penniman's students were meeting the real needs of a nonprofit organization that works in Haiti, where the teacher has family ties. The use of solar ovens is an affordable, sustainable alternative to cooking with charcoal, which contributes to deforestation and creates health risks for those who breathe in smoke.

Launching the project

Penniman launched the project by sharing a letter with students, in which the nonprofit president explained why he needed their help:

> *We are always looking for more efficient and affordable solar oven designs. To that end, we would like you to design a parabolic trough solar oven for potential use in our Haiti program. We will send our representatives to review your designs mid-project and to see your "pitch presentations" at the end of the project. Our interest is in an affordable, compact oven and container that is effective in capturing the sun's energy. In addition to the prototype oven, we ask that you organize a spec sheet including your designs, calculations, and justifications so that our engineers can replicate and further develop your work.*

Building knowledge and skills

Few students have prior experiences with PBL before arriving at Tech Valley High, a public school that draws students from a large region. That's why Penniman takes a deliberate approach to introducing her ninth graders to processes that foster innovative thinking and problem solving.

For example, students learn to quickly sketch out their rough ideas (by hand or using digital tools like SketchUp) so that they can make their thinking visible and get feedback on their ideas. Penniman expects each team to generate and do preliminary research on at least three ideas before they move ahead with prototyping and testing one of them. She also teaches students how to build consensus, so that the whole team can get behind the idea they decide to develop. Students learn to use the critical friends protocol (described in Chapter 3: Collaboration), which guides them to make improvements based on "I like..." and "I wonder..." feedback from peers and experts.

> Students learn to quickly sketch out their rough ideas so that they can make their thinking visible and get feedback on their ideas.

What does this look like in practice? Here's how Penniman describes the teaching and learning that unfolds in her PBL classroom:

> *Early in the project, there's a lot happening. Student teams are doing research and presenting what they find out to make sure everyone understands the concepts. Teachers are giving workshops, which are short, interactive lectures to build content knowledge.*

For this interdisciplinary project, Penniman knew that students would have to apply their understanding of algebra and materials science, along with creativity. She consulted with engineers to make sure that the project would be do-able given the kind of math students would need to understand and apply. She knew that if the ovens used a parabolic trough feature to collect solar energy, then students would need to think about quadratic equations, roots, and focal points. That made sense at the Algebra I or II level, which meant the design challenge was academically right-sized for her students.

To help students build understanding of key concepts, Penniman prompted students "to ask the right questions so we could teach them the math and science they need to know," she explains. For math, that involved questions relating to quadratics. Science standards addressed by the project included an introduction to the properties of materials (such as conductivity, reflectivity, malleability, cost), as well as environmental science concepts involving deforestation.

A "fail fast" attitude encourages innovation in a variety of real-world settings.

Developing products

While she is emphasizing academic content, Penniman also works at overcoming one of the biggest barriers to creativity: students' fear of failure. "The main thing that prevents students from being creative is a fear of being penalized if they make mistakes," she says, "so we look at ways to reward making mistakes." A similar "fail fast" attitude encourages innovation in a variety of real-world settings, from engineering and design labs to product development teams. Facebook, for example, is known for the motto, "Move fast. Break stuff."

In the classroom, Penniman reinforces a fail-safe culture by taking grades out of the equation while students are generating, testing, and refining ideas. Ungraded formative assessment is much more frequent in her classroom than summative assessment. When it's time for final assessment and grading, she uses a rubric to weigh student work against a variety of criteria. "It's not just, did the product come out well? We assess the problem-solving process, their critical thinking, how they did on oral presentation." When grades reflect several indicators, she says, "each component becomes lower stakes. That seems to free students up to think more creatively."

The solar ovens project also gave students practical experience with what Penniman calls "creativity within constraints." Students had to address specific design requirements while keeping within a tight budget for materials. If they came up with efficient but affordable designs, their nonprofit client might be able to expand its product line and better meet the needs of Haitian families. "We weren't sure if the parabolic trough would be an improvement over existing designs," she adds, "but we wanted to experiment with a new way of thinking to find out."

As student teams worked on product development, they used an iterative cycle to improve their designs. Penniman explains, "Mid-project, you're going to see teams drawing designs, refining them, exploring different materials in the workshop area, and redesigning." This is also the time when she invited guest experts — in this case, engineers — to critique students' rough drafts. She describes what happened:

> We put all the rough drafts up on the overhead and the engineers asked critical questions. They really treated students like fellow engineers (and didn't hesitate to lovingly tear their designs apart!). One team, for example, had an excellent design, but they hadn't considered the position of the sun. The engineers said, "OK, where do you think the sun will be located at the time of day when people would be using the ovens? Have you created a sun-ray diagram? Have you calculated the focal point?" Using this feedback, students could then go back and refine their designs.

As the project deadline approached, student teams scrambled to finalize and test what they had built, and also prepared their final reports and presentations.

Presenting products

The same engineers who critiqued the rough drafts returned at the end of the project when students made their "pitch" presentations. Teams assembled all their project information, including written reports and documentation from lab tests, and delivered oral presentations about the benefits of their oven designs. This information was also shared with the nonprofit organization in Haiti, which planned to run field tests of some of the most promising student designs.

Although the presentations marked the end of the project (and it was time for final grading based on a project rubric), Penniman left the door open for more student creativity. Students were free to revise their oven designs, even months after the due date. Penniman says this open-ended revision policy invites students to continue thinking about product improvements and to take more creative risks.

Bulletin Board

Research Spotlight: PBL Teachers Scaffold Creativity

An important part of building competence in creativity and innovation is having students generate their own ideas about how to confront a problem or question. The majority (65%) of teachers who use PBL ask students to do this at least weekly; only 35% of teachers who do not use PBL do this weekly.

Students should also be taught to use idea-creation techniques such as brainstorming or concept mapping. Almost half (42%) of teachers who use PBL ask students to do this at least once a week; only 24% of teachers who do not use PBL do this weekly.

Source: Hixson, Ravitz, and Whisman, 2012

Your Turn: Design, Develop, and Determine

To teach and assess creativity in PBL, use a three-part approach:

Design

At the design stage, look for projects that will challenge students to create original products or design solutions that serve an authentic, valuable purpose for an intended audience. Help them imagine where the project might lead. Will students be challenged to come up with an invention or new product, or improve on an existing product? Will they devise a process for solving or addressing a local (or global) issue? Will they publish their writing in an illustrated book or present a poetry slam to an audience? Will they be remixing digital content to make new meaning? Are their products likely to integrate the arts? To arrive at any of these end results, students will need to put their creativity and innovation to work.

> Look for projects that will challenge students to create original products or design solutions that serve an authentic, valuable purpose for an intended audience.

In Chapter 4, we heard how English learners in Amy Carrington's class put their problem solving and communication skills to work to improve access to Spanish-language books at the community library. In another project, the same students applied creative thinking to produce a documentary. Carrington explains how the project came about: "Our community has a large Hispanic population. Our English language students said they wanted to do a project about workplace issues facing Hispanic people. They teamed up with a high school film class and did video interviews of parents, factory workers, employers from our area." Their final product was an artfully produced documentary about workplace issues and workers' rights that students screened in a red-carpet event for the community.

To encourage students' creativity and innovative thinking, consider projects that involve:

Design and invention challenges

- How might we improve a playground design to promote children's fitness?
- How can we use scrap materials to improve wildlife habitat on our school campus?
- How can we improve outdoor experiences for people with disabilities?
- How can we design a monument to Vietnam War veterans that honors all points of view in our community?

Problem-solving

- How should we advise a local lottery winner to invest her winnings for long-term gains?

- What is the best location for the next state park?

- How can we deal with invasive species in our waterways?

- How can we help make recent immigrants a part of our community?

Arts integration

- What stories does graffiti tell about our community?

- How can we create a work of art or media that celebrates our cultural and/or community heritage?

- How can we use digital gaming to reduce our carbon footprint?

Identify constraints

The design stage is also the time to consider practicalities. How much time do you want to spend on the project? Which content standards do you plan to address? Will all student teams create the same product, or different products — and will the products be specified in advance, or will students come up with their own ideas? Your answers will determine whether the project design is more open-ended or more constrained.

In the solar ovens example, the project began with an existing problem and well-crafted Driving Question: How can we improve the design of solar ovens to benefit people living in poor conditions in Haiti? As teacher Leah Penniman explained, she gave students specific constraints, such as a cap on the cost of materials they could use and requirement to incorporate a parabolic trough. "Creativity within constraints" helped to keep

> Will the products be specified in advance, or will students come up with their own ideas?

the focus on specific math and science standards. Such design specifications are authentic. In engineering, design, computer science, architecture, and many other fields, professionals typically have to work creatively within constraints.

Another teacher, however, might have come at the topic of deforestation and poverty quite differently. Instead of starting with solar ovens, what if you wanted students to think more broadly about what they could do to improve the lives of people living in poorly resourced regions? In a global studies and geography project, you might begin by introducing students to the UN Millennium Development Goals. Using statistics, students could compare the quality of life in many countries and not limit their focus to Haiti. This background-building would likely happen before a Driving Question is even written. In fact, you might want to involve students in writing and refining the Driving Question, once they have invested time to understand the global issue of poverty and identify the specific issue they want to address. Presented with a more open-ended project design, students might suggest and develop a wide range of possible solutions — with solar ovens just one of many possible products, and Haiti one of many contexts. Depending on the direction students decide to take, the project could integrate social studies, math, and science, along with writing across the curriculum.

Although these two examples differ in scope, time commitment, and academic content, both put a deliberate emphasis on thinking creatively to generate, refine, and advocate for solutions.

Ask students to discuss: Are innovators born or made?

Develop

As you prepare to launch the project, make sure students understand what creativity means and why being able to apply this 21st century competency is going to serve them well in college, careers, and life.

To develop students' creative capabilities throughout a project, anticipate key issues and be ready with additional supports, as needed. Use the following guidelines to help you create a classroom culture that supports creativity, build students' understanding of what it means to be creative and innovative, and provide scaffolding when needed.

Foster a creative culture

If your students are less familiar with innovation and creativity, take time early in the project (or even before project launch) to define these important concepts and encourage them as part of your classroom culture. Lead a class discussion about creativity and innovation. For example, you might ask students to generate a list of examples of people being creative in any endeavor, from mainstream media (advertising or music videos) to personal expression (locker art or clothing styles). Take the discussion deeper by asking students to discuss: Are innovators born or made?

Some schools emphasize creativity and innovation goals across the curriculum. That's the case at Tech Valley High, where students begin hearing about innovation and creative problem solving from their first day as ninth graders. "I'm not sure they see innovation as any different from written communication or technology literacy. It's just the air they breathe here," Penniman observes.

To encourage everyone to be creative, be ready to challenge students' tendency to label themselves as creative types — or not. Students may mistakenly

Practice "Plussing"

At Pixar Animation Studio, employees use a process known as "plussing" to improve on creative ideas. Instead of simply shooting down someone's idea, every criticism must be followed by a "plus" — a better idea. Plussing means asking, "How can I take someone else's idea and make it even better?" Teach your students how to harness the power of plussing.

For example, ask students to imagine they work for an amusement park and start the process by offering them an idea such as "let's create a new thrill ride based on Harry Potter that looks like Hogwarts castle." The next person to contribute must accept this idea and build upon it by saying something like, "YES, and what if it has other locations too like the forest with the spiders and the Ministry of Magic?" The third person then builds further saying, "YES, and the sound track should have the voices of the main characters."

assume that they aren't creative if they lack natural talent in music or drawing. Challenge their thinking by pointing out creativity isn't fixed at birth but gets better with practice. Help them understand that creative thinking extends in many directions and isn't limited to the arts. Share examples of innovators from diverse fields and from different time periods, and ask students to consider the factors that have contributed to their success. Remind students that creative efforts often result from the application of the same strategies that they will learn. Tell students about the opportunities they will have during the project to develop and demonstrate their own creativity.

To reinforce the idea that everyone has creative potential, ask students to think about when they feel most creative. Where are they? What are they doing? What does it feel like to generate ideas? How might they bring this creative spark into their project work? This is also an opportunity to model a classroom culture that makes it safe for students to express their ideas without fear of ridicule or put-downs.

Share a rubric — or co-create one with students — that captures what it means to think creatively and use innovation processes. Be sure the rubric uses student-friendly language. (See **Useful Stuff** for an example.)

Learn From Innovators

There are many resources for learning more about innovators and creative problem solvers. For example:

- Odyssey of the Mind (**odysseyofthemind.com**) includes mini-profiles of creative people along with classroom activities to encourage creativity.

- On Innovation (**oninnovation.com**) includes interviews with well-known innovators from today and historical accounts of yesterday's creative thinkers.

- Maker Faire (**makerfaire.com**), which started as a grassroots festival of creativity in arts, craft, engineering, technology, and other fields, has grown into an international movement that celebrates do-it-yourself (DIY) innovation, often on a low budget. The Maker Faire community now includes Maker Faires around the world and Maker Clubs in K-12 settings, where students tackle DIY projects of their own design.

Emphasize processes for innovation

Good ideas seldom come out of thin air. That's why, in projects that emphasize creativity and innovation, you want to introduce students to processes and strategies for generating and developing creative solutions. Look for opportunities to encourage creative thinking and innovation at every stage of PBL.

When you launch the project, help students understand the reason for doing it by prompting them to consider these questions as they generate a Need to Know list: Who will be served by this project? What need or issue is currently going unmet? What do we know about our intended audience? Who struggles with this problem every day (and could provide insights from the user's point of view)?

Help students expand their perspective about an issue by:

- Conducting interviews or hosting focus groups to learn from people whose lives are affected by the issue

- Doing field research or observations to "see" the problem with their own eyes

- Taking surveys to learn more about their audience's attitudes and perspectives

In the solar ovens project, students learned about the issues of deforestation and poverty from their nonprofit client in Haiti, as well as from experts who served as project consultants. Investing time to understand the problem from multiple perspectives not only yields better solutions, but also helps students develop empathy for others' perspectives — another trait that's common among innovators.

As you build knowledge and skills, use a variety of teaching strategies to help students understand both the academic content and the creative challenges of the project. In the solar ovens example, students learned about math and science concepts and also learned processes for making their thinking visible with rough sketches and prototyping.

As students develop products, they may need to make repeat cycles through the steps of generating ideas, prototyping, and improving their creative work in response to critical feedback. Allow plenty of time in the project calendar for this iterative approach to product development.

Scaffold students' creative thinking

Throughout the "Develop" stage, teach students to use strategies such as the ones listed below that will help them generate original ideas or solutions, as well as build on each other's ideas. Share with them the strategies that experts use to generate, evaluate, and apply ideas that have creative merit.

> Share the strategies that experts use to generate, evaluate, and apply ideas that have creative merit.

- **Brainstorm better:** Instead of just turning students loose to "brainstorm with your team," teach them to make the most of this process. Remind them that the goal of brainstorming is to build an idea bank — the more, the better. Creativity experts call this abundance of ideas creative fluency. (See Bulletin Board, Tips for Better Brainstorming, on page 101.)

- **Learn to brainwrite:** As an alternative to brainstorming, try "brainwriting" to produce a number of ideas in a short time. Once again, the goal is to generate as many ideas as possible in response to a specific problem or question. Each student in a circle starts with a sheet of paper with the brainwriting topic at the top. Give students a few minutes to write down one or two suggestions, then pass the paper to the next student. Students read what's on the sheet and then respond by adding two more ideas (or elaborations on previous suggestions). They continue this process until they receive their original paper back. It should be filled with ideas that the team can now evaluate as a group.

- **Try SCAMPER:** Teach students to use the SCAMPER strategy when they are developing products or processes. SCAMPER, a widely used technique credited to educator Robert Eberle, involves asking a series of questions to improve on a product or concept. Each letter in the mnemonic stands for a different question to consider:

Substitute: Which materials or components could you substitute, swap, or change to make something work better? (Think of improving a laptop by swapping the display for a touch screen.)

Combine: Can you imagine mashing up two or more products or ideas to create something new? (Think of all the functions that are combined in a Swiss Army knife or smart phone.)

Adapt: Can you adapt this product or idea to serve a new purpose? (Think of a channel on YouTube with content just for education, or a case for an e-book reader that converts to a stand.)

Modify: Are there elements you can tweak or modify to add value? (Picture an exercise bike that captures user-generated energy.)

Put to another use: Who else could use this product or idea? What new purposes could it serve? (Think of a product like Velcro, used in early aerospace missions, which now has widespread applications in consumer products.)

Eliminate: What features could you get rid of to make this even better? (Think of keyless ignitions for cars, or streamlined processes for applying for college admission.)

Reverse: What if this did just the opposite of what it does now? (Imagine a washing machine that also dries clothes or a savings card that works like a credit card in reverse.)

If these ways of thinking are new to students, introduce them to SCAMPER with a whole-class discussion in which they improve upon something familiar, such as school assemblies or a binder. How might students make assemblies more engaging or a give a binder more uses by applying SCAMPER? Once they understand the basic steps of SCAMPER, they will be ready to apply this thinking process to improve their own products.

- **Practice prototyping:** Teach students to represent their rough ideas using a variety of methods — such as sketching, modeling, storyboarding, role-playing, or acting out with a short sketch or dialogue. If students are developing physical objects, provide them with materials and space to tinker. If they are unfamiliar with making models or prototypes, do some skill-building activities to introduce them to various tools or technologies, or have students with expertise teach their peers. Remind students that the goal of prototyping is to make an idea visible so that others can respond to it. Feedback at this early stage will lead to better final products.

> The goal of prototyping is to make an idea visible so that others can respond to it.

Bulletin Board — Tips for Better Brainstorming

The brainstorming process emerged from the advertising industry decades ago and is now widely used in fields ranging from engineering and product design to social problem solving. IDEO, a global design firm, relies on these seven rules to encourage creative, high-energy, group-thinking sessions:

1. Defer judgment
2. Encourage wild ideas
3. Build on the ideas of others
4. Stay focused on the topic
5. One conversation at a time
6. Be visual
7. Go for quantity

(Read more about IDEO's celebrated brainstorming process at **openideo.com**).

What happens if your students quickly exhaust their ideas during a brainstorming session? Try these tips to get the creative juices flowing:

- **Give students time to come up with some ideas individually before brainstorming with their team.** This runs counter to traditional brainstorming, which puts a premium on the creative energy of small groups. But extra thinking time may be especially helpful for quieter students and English learners. They can make notes to refer back to during active brainstorming sessions when the conversation tends to move quickly. Researchers have found that getting people to think individually about a topic before combining their ideas can be more productive than starting out thinking as a group (Kohn & Smith, 2010). As a variation, have teams pause their brainstorming session to allow for individual think time. After a few minutes, regroup to see what new ideas have emerged.

- **When students start generating ideas as a group, encourage them to actively discuss suggestions** (without dismissing anyone's ideas). Once again, this is a break from traditional brainstorming practice. But the back-and-forth can stimulate even more ideas, especially if students are drawing on diverse perspectives and backgrounds. Beyond the classroom, good ideas often result at the edges or intersections of disciplines. That's why workplaces known for creativity deliberately create opportunities for employees to cross paths — both formally and informally — to build on or challenge each other's thinking.

- **Be sure that students gather every suggestion that comes up in their discussions** (for example, have students summarize each of their own ideas on a sticky note or mind map, or have someone from another team be their idea recorder). A suggestion that might not be the leading contender at first may be worth a second look after students do more research and analysis, or start to develop prototypes.

- **If students seem stuck or give up after offering just one idea, encourage them to keep going.** Try responding to their initial suggestion with, "Yes, and (what else)?" It's a way to recognize their contribution while nudging them to persist.

- **If students have trouble explaining their ideas, teach them strategies to make their thinking visible.** Using rough sketches, concept maps, or a few key words, they can capture an idea before it gets away. Remind them that ideas need to move from one person's imagination into the open, where they can be discussed, debated, tested, evaluated, and improved upon. Share examples of products or services that started with "back-of-the-envelope" or cocktail napkin sketches, such as village banking and the Pregnant Guppy cargo plane.

Inexpensive versions of 3-D printers are making their way to K-12 classrooms, providing students with a new way to prototype their ideas. The next generation of digital fabricators are small enough to sit on a desktop; a special version for education is in development. Just as a laser printer follows your computer's commands to print documents, 3-D printers follow digital commands to "print" objects by putting down layers of wax, plastic, even Play-Doh! For students, 3-D printers offer a fast-track way to take a raw idea from the mind's eye to real life (Boss, 2012). Stay up-to-date on developments by following Fab@Home, an open-source community of professionals and hobbyists. Learn more at **fabathome.org**.

Use formative assessment, critique, and revision

Be deliberate about checking in with students about the creative aspects of their projects. As a practical strategy, have students keep design notebooks, research journals, or blogs in which they reflect on their progress. These project records capture students' thinking over the course of the project (including the self-criticism that can inhibit creativity). Review these documents at scheduled check-ins to offer constructive feedback and encouragement specifically related to the creative aspects of the project.

When students are critiquing and revising products, provide them with feedback forms or protocols that will elicit useful, specific peer feedback about creativity. For example, you might ask reviewers to consider:

- **Originality:** Have you ever seen a product or suggestion like this before? Does it remind you of anything else?

- **Functionality:** Could this idea really work, or it is pie-in-the-sky thinking? What bugs might need to be worked out before it could be used?

- **Ingenuity:** How does this idea improve on existing solutions? For example, is it faster, smaller, cheaper, greener, or easier to make than alternatives?

- **Beauty/Elegance**: Does it look good? Is it elegant or clever in its design? Does the writing/artwork/piece of media have features that make it exceptional?

TIP FROM THE CLASSROOM

Ask students to create slogans.

Challenge students to come up their own reminders that encourage risk-taking and learning from failure. For example, one teacher encourages his students to allow themselves to fail, but, "don't fail the same way twice." Have students take part in a brainstorming session about how to make your classroom a space that encourages learning from failure. Encourage them to be specific — and creative. For example, if they suggest being non-judgmental about each other's ideas, ask them to turn that concept into a slogan.

Think Like an Architect: Plan a Charrette

Charrette is a process for promoting public participation in the creative design process. Used by architects and urban planners, the process depends on active collaboration and feedback from stakeholders to improve ideas in a group setting. For example, plans for a new school building might kick off with a design *charrette* that involves teachers, students, parents, and other community members working alongside architects, engineers, and others with specialized expertise. Learn more about the charrette process from the National Charrette Institute (**charretteinstitute.org**).

Troubleshoot creativity and innovation challenges

Once the project is underway, spend time observing student teams at work, asking questions, listening to their discussions, and using other formative assessment tools and strategies. If you notice students struggling when it comes to creative thinking, be ready with just-in-time help or redirection.

If students see some of their ideas fail when developing products, encourage them to analyze and learn from failure and set-backs. Innovators and creative types don't give up when an idea doesn't pan out. They use their insights from these situations to inform their next attempt at a solution. Build and reinforce a classroom culture that makes it safe to attempt novel ideas.

If students do not seem to be coming up with creative ideas, incorporate checkpoints and progress reports when they are developing products or prototypes. Check-ins and milestones are important for project management, and should be included in all projects. Especially in projects that emphasize creativity and innovation, however, students may need extra help developing what experts call "creative confidence." This is the confidence to take risks and offer novel ideas. Fear of criticism—or worry about giving the wrong answer—can hamper creative confidence well into adulthood.

If you feel that you can't provide adequate support on your own, bring in an outside expert to help students troubleshoot a challenge. Or try having students present their problem to the whole class and ask for suggestions. Help students recognize that they are building the habits of mind—risk-taking, persistence, optimism—that innovators share. Share real-world examples of how professionals across different fields work through challenges. For

Define Creative Competence

Have students listen to David Kelley, founder of the global design firm IDEO, talk about creative confidence in his TED Talk at **ted.com**. Have students define "creative confidence" in their own words. Discuss the question, What helps them feel this way?

example, architects host design *charrettes* to solicit ideas from multiple stakeholders; technologists tackle programming challenges during intense *hackathons*.

Determine

At the end of the project, when students present products and share (and perhaps defend or explain) their work with an audience, put your summative assessment plan into action. For projects that emphasize creativity and innovation, you will need to assess both content mastery and the creativity or innovation demonstrated in the project.

Assessing creativity can be a tricky proposition. You may question whether it's fair to measure creativity at all. Concerns about cultural bias and subjectivity naturally arise when it comes to assessing creative work. History is replete with examples of artists and writers whose work was not appreciated in their lifetime, or whose creative products fell out of favor when times and trends changed. You may also wonder if you're sending conflicting or even harmful messages by grading students on creative thinking. Would a poor score undermine students' creative confidence, leading them to conclude, "I'm just not the creative type"? Is it a mixed message to encourage student to "learn from failure" and "think outside the box," but then assign a score to their work?

These concerns are not limited to the classroom. Susan Besemer, an author and expert on assessing creativity in product design, cautions against critical feedback that feels "heavy—like taking a sledgehammer to an idea." (Arnold, n.d.) To counter subjectivity and make room for more productive feedback, she developed a three-dimensional model for assessing creativity in any number of products. She suggests assessing novelty (is the product new or unique, surprising or original?), resolution (does it solve a defined problem or address a need?), and style (does it synthesize disparate elements into a coherent, well-crafted whole?). The same questions are worth asking as you develop project rubrics to use with students. The "Product" section of the Creativity & Innovation Rubric for PBL found in **Useful Stuff** reflects Besemer's model.

Here are additional considerations to help you think about what and how to assess when it comes to creativity.

Be clear at the outset about how student work will be assessed for creativity. The rubric or scoring guide that you shared with students (or wrote together with them) near the beginning of the project should clearly explain your criteria for assessing creative thinking. For example, the Creativity & Innovation Rubric for PBL in **Useful Stuff** describes the extent to which a product demonstrates originality, value, and style, as well as describing the quality of the innovation process used to create the product.

Be ready to explain how you arrived at your standards for assessing creativity. For example, have you consulted with experts, as Penniman did for the solar ovens project? Are you drawing on your own understanding of a discipline that you have studied in depth, such as art or architecture?

Make sure students understand the criteria, and also help them understand that there is room for a wide range of responses that meet these goals. Share student work samples for students to critique, using your scoring guide. Be sure to offer a range of samples so that students can imagine many creative approaches in their own work.

In your assessment language, emphasize the process along with the product. For example, Penniman's rubric for the solar ovens project was specific about expectations for how students should use feedback: "Solar collector design improves in response to feedback in the mid-project critique."

Similarly, an online project asked students to creatively tackle some of the world's biggest problems. Their proposed solutions to the UN Millennium Development Goals were expected to be tangible, pragmatic, and make-able, and students were expected to explain their thinking with prototypes at a showcase event. That set the stage for assessment that focused on how well students could explain their proposed solution, including how they had arrived at it and why they thought it would be useful for addressing the Millennium Development Goals. (Read more about the ITU Telecom World 11: The Youth Metaconference at **notosh.com).**

If you want to encourage students to take creative risks, consider divergent ideas, and be open to others' perspectives, emphasize these behaviors in your assessment language. Ask students to provide evidence (such as reflections or project journals) that they have applied these strategies as part of their project work.

> Describe the extent to which a product demonstrates originality, value, and style, as well as the quality of the innovation process used to create the product.

Welcome authentic feedback. When students present their products, they will gain valuable feedback if the audience includes people who would benefit from their proposed solutions or products. Have students reflect on these authentic reactions. For example, ask students: If you had time to keep going with this idea, how would you revise your product or solution to make it even better at meeting your audience's needs?

TIP FROM THE CLASSROOM

Include a Breakthrough on a Rubric

Be ready to acknowledge truly game-changing ideas if and when they occur. PBL advocate Thom Markham suggests teachers include a "breakthrough" category on project rubrics. "The breakthrough column goes beyond the A, rewarding innovation, creativity, and something new outside the formal curriculum. It's a show-me category," he explains (Markham, 2010). Before adding a breakthrough column, think about how you will recognize this level of exceptional performance. What would students need to make, do, or show? Experts from related disciplines could help you by offering real-life examples of breakthrough thinking in their fields. Help students understand that breakthroughs are rare — but worth celebrating when they happen (Boss, 2012).

TECH TIP Tools to Encourage Innovation
and Creativity

Digital tools open new opportunities for students to engage in creative problem solving and expression.

For example:

- **SketchUp** (formerly a Google tool) is an online drawing tool for making 3D models. Students can use it to make visual representation of ideas at the brainstorming or prototyping stage. A free version is available for K-12 education. Learn more at **sketchup.com**.

- **Skitch** is an app that allows you to make digital sketches, add annotation, and manipulate screenshots, and then share your work digitally. Students might use it for annotating rough sketches, exchanging feedback at the idea stage, or building on others' ideas. Learn more at **evernote.com**.

- **Glogster** (glogster.com) is a site for producing and publishing interactive posters, or graphic blogs. Students can use Glogster to combine a variety of digital content about a project. Glogs can be embedded on blogs or shared on social networks. GlogsterEdu (**edu.glogster.com**) is a social network specifically designed for the education community.

- **Bubbl.us**, **SpiderScribe**, and **mySimpleSurface** (all free) are three of the many online tools available for brainstorming, mind-mapping, and organizing creative ideas.

Creativity and Innovation Throughout a Project

with Common Core Alignment

- ▶ Students make sure they understand the purpose driving the process of innovation by asking, who needs this and why?

- ▶ When students ask follow-up questions that focus or broaden the inquiry (CC ELA 6-12.W.7) they develop insight about the particular needs and interests of the target audience.

- ▶ When students gather information to address the Driving Question from multiple and varied sources (CC ELA 6,11-12.RI.7) they find unusual sources of information or develop innovative methods for gathering it.

- ▶ Students promote divergent and creative perspectives during discussions. (CC ELA 11-12.SL.1c)

Launching the Project

An engaging Entry Event and open-ended Driving Question launch students on their inquiry experience. Need to Know discussions raise questions that will guide students' investigation.

Building Knowledge, Understanding and Skills

Students learn necessary content knowledge from the teacher, readings, and other resources, and gain skills that will help them create project products and answer the Driving Question. They do research, test hypotheses, and gather and analyze data.

Developing and Revising Ideas and Products

Students consider diverse perspectives and generate multiple solutions, designs, and answers to the Driving Question. Through cycles of critical feedback, they refine their thinking and improve on early ideas as they create final products.

▶ Students use a variety of strategies to generate original ideas or solutions, evaluate them, then select the best one to shape into an original product or answer to the Driving Question.

▶ Students seek out and use feedback and critique to improve products. (CC ELA 6-8.W.5)

▶ Students persevere in solving problems, monitoring and evaluating their progress and changing course, if necessary. (CC Math 6-12.Math Practices.1)

Presenting Products and Answers to Driving Questions

Students share the results of their efforts with a public audience, demonstrating what they learned in the project. They explain and defend their research, product design, and strategies for problem solving. Finally, they reflect on their experience.

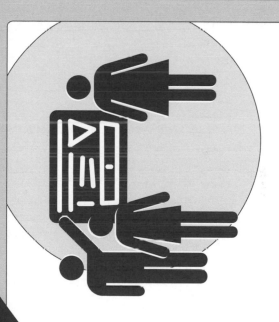

▶ When students create presentation media and visual displays (CC ELA 6-12.SL.5) they make them visually exciting and include creative design touches.

▶ Students include elements in their presentation that are especially fun, lively, engaging, or powerful for the audience.

For Parents and Other Community Stakeholders:

Top 10 Reasons Why Teaching 21st Century Competencies via PBL is a Good Idea*

1. Our graduates will be better prepared for college and careers.

2. Students will still learn academic content (and remember it better).

3. Our test scores will be fine, and our students will be better able to meet the new Common Core State Standards.

4. Your children will get better at managing their time and staying organized.

5. Students will learn how to work together to get things done, just as they will need to do on the job.

6. Students' public presentations will be fun to watch, and give them a chance to develop communication skills.

7. Your kids will be more engaged and take more responsibility for their own learning.

8. Students' creativity might lead to improvements in our community.

9. You can share what you know as a content expert, guest speaker, or project consultant.

10. Your kids will have interesting things to say when you ask, "What did you do in school today?"

*To learn more about the research supporting PBL, see PBL Research Summary in **Useful Stuff.**

BUILDING SUPPORT FOR 21ST CENTURY LEARNING

Because PBL is still relatively new in many communities, few adults have seen this approach to teaching and learning in action. You can bet that doing 21st century learning projects is not the way most parents and community members "did school" when they were younger.

When you introduce new strategies to help students develop their 21st century competencies, don't be surprised if parents and other community members express their own need to know questions about what's going on in the classroom. Some may wonder how non-academic skills like communication or creativity will help students get into college. Parents who are unfamiliar with collaborative projects might question the fairness of team grades or ask why students aren't getting the kind of homework assignments they are used to seeing.

To alleviate potential concerns and build a positive culture for PBL, classroom teachers, administrators, and school board members all play important roles in communicating why schools need to emphasize 21st century competencies. Students, too, tend to make excellent ambassadors for school change. By sharing their project experiences and problem-solving strategies publicly, they offer adults a look at what 21st century learners can accomplish by tackling academically rigorous projects.

This chapter offers four strategies to build community support for 21st century learning. Dialogues with stakeholders offer opportunities to enlist parents, members of the business and nonprofit community, and others as active partners in student learning. We have included additional resources to help you facilitate those conversations, such as the "Top 10" list on page 110. You can also find a helpful resource, Frequently Asked Questions about PBL, in **Useful Stuff**.

Strategies for Building Community Support

1. Engage parents as allies.

Help parents understand the value of 21st century competencies to support their children's success in college and careers. Although it's true that PBL is different from the way most parents experienced school, projects reflect the way that important work gets done in the real world. Most parents have had firsthand experience with projects in their careers and community activities. Help them make the connection between the competencies that their students are developing today and the challenges they will need to be ready to face in the future.

Bulletin Board

PBL Will Help Students and Schools Meet Common Core Expectations

As states and local districts begin to implement the Common Core State Standards, schools have an opportunity to help community members anticipate the changes ahead. Parents and business leaders will likely want to know: What do these new standards mean for our students? How are you preparing our students to meet these higher expectations for learning?

This is an opportunity to show how PBL, with an emphasis on 21st century competencies, prepares students to do more than fill in the right bubble on standardized tests. Unlike the assessments many community members are familiar with after a decade of *No Child Left Behind* testing, the next-generation assessments are expected to measure how well students can apply what they know. Pilot tasks in development by the Partnership for Assessment of Readiness for College and Career, or PARCC, and the Smarter Balanced Assessment Consortium emphasize performance assessments. A sample pilot assessment task developed by Smarter Balanced, for instance, asks 11th graders to "engage strategically in collaborative and independent inquiry to investigate/research topics, pose questions, and gather and present information." Help community members notice the phrases that align with 21st century learning, such as "strategically" (calling for critical thinking), "collaborative," and "present information" (calling on communication competencies). The call for "inquiry" and "posing questions" also reflects best practices in PBL.

Schools that emphasize PBL as a core instructional strategy typically offer open houses, school tours, and other informative events to help parents understand the project approach. Many PBL teachers adopt an open-door policy that invites visitors to drop in and take a look at projects in action. Such activities help to build a school culture that supports PBL, as this teacher explains:

We preach from day one during parent orientation and open house that we are preparing their kids for their future careers...I love to hear parents say, "I wish school was like this when I was a kid!" The true value of PBL should be "modeled" to parents by students and teachers through effectively using oral and written communication and collaboration. The parents will become disciples when they see the growth and passion for learning in their children.

Don't expect to reset expectations or create a new school culture with a one-time event. Engage parents and other community members in an ongoing conversation about 21st century learning and welcome their contributions to students' success with these practical strategies:

> Don't expect to reset expectations or create a new school culture with a one-time event.

- **Guide discussions:** Using your school website, social media, and other communications channels, share research, readings, and videos to help parents understand the opportunities offered by 21st century learning. For example, school leaders might suggest titles and discussion questions for parent book clubs. (See Appendix for suggested readings.) Share the "PBL Explained" video at **bie.org**, which offers a succinct, animated explanation.

- **Send letters home:** Keep parents informed about students' projects. When teachers launch a new project, share expectations with parents by sending home a letter (via email, website or Facebook post, or other form of communication likely to reach your parent community) that outlines the learning goals (both content and 21st century competencies), assessment plan, important due dates, and opportunities for parent involvement.

- **Use tech tools:** Use technology tools to give parents a real-time view of student learning. Online tools like Edmodo, a social network for education, or Project Foundry, a project management platform, allow you to invite parents to view project workspaces. If your students are blogging as part of a project, for example, invite parents to comment on student posts. One teacher in a PBL-oriented school prepares parents to comment on student blogs by hosting an evening event where parents test-drive tech tools, learn protocols for giving positive feedback, and practice writing blog comments.

- **Share expertise:** Encourage parents to contribute to projects by taking part in focus groups or surveys, serving as subject-area experts, or providing feedback on presentations. Early in the year, find out about parents' areas of expertise by taking a survey or creating a Google doc. Tap their subject-area knowledge, as needed, by inviting them to consult with students or assess student work (formatively or during final presentations).

- **Recruit "project parents":** If your school has active parent volunteers, recruit a "project parent" (instead of a room parent) to help arrange student transportation, chaperone students doing field research, or help with other logistics that may involve student work outside the classroom. Connect with your parent-teacher association to keep parents informed about opportunities to support PBL.

- **Student-led conferences**: Bring students into parent-teacher conferences. These events may require more preparation to get students ready, but offer rich opportunities for conversation and reflection. Encourage students to use conference time to describe their own growth, challenges, and goals as learners, using project work samples as illustrations. There is a good video from Washington Heights Expeditionary Learning School on student-led conferences at **vimeo.com/45140230** and their handbook is available at **goo.gl/7c7Bv**.

2. Connect with community experts and supporters.

The in-depth inquiry that's a hallmark of PBL often takes students beyond the classroom to gather research or consult with subject-area experts. This opens more opportunities for community engagement.

- **Establish a project advisory board:** School leaders may want to establish an advisory board for PBL. Invite participation by representatives from the business community, higher education, government, and others who have a stake in developing a pipeline of young people ready to tackle future challenges. Give advisers a close-up look at student work by inviting them to consult with students or provide expert feedback at showcase events.

- **Tap content-area experts:** Develop ongoing relationships with content-area experts, including parents, representatives of nonprofit and business organizations, faculty from local colleges and community colleges, school counselors, and others with expertise to share. Don't overlook current college students and graduate students, along with hobbyists or do-it-yourselfers (such as participants in "hackerspaces" or DIY events like Maker Faire). In the chapter on creativity, for example, you heard how a teacher asked for help from engineers on a solar ovens project. You might solicit similar help from student chapters of engineering societies. When inviting experts to consult on projects, be specific about the help you are seeking and the time involved.

> If your school has active parent volunteers, recruit a "project parent" (instead of a room parent) to help with logistics

You'll likely find that community members are eager to help, if they have a clear understanding of what's required and the expected time commitment.

■ **Recruit community clients:** Establish ongoing relationships with nonprofit organizations, local businesses, or others that can benefit from students' 21st century competencies. Encourage organizations to share problems or issues that could benefit from student problem solving. For example, students might use their critical thinking and communication skills to help a nonprofit organization develop public-service announcements, or create website content to help businesses attract more customers.

■ **Connect with business and industry:** Local employers concerned about workforce readiness are likely to be strong advocates for developing students' 21st century competencies. Businesses employ a wide range of experts who may be interested in consulting with students or serving on a project judging panel. Your local chamber of commerce can be a good starting point for making connections.

■ **Reach out to the community:** Take advantage of your district's community engagement experts to build relationships with local organizations and potential partners. Share student success stories through your district's media relations channels. One teacher, for example, makes a point of inviting media representatives to project showcase events. Students gain positive press for their efforts and also engage in authentic reflection when interviewed about what they have learned.

3. Engage students as ambassadors.

Not surprisingly, students are often the best advocates for the rich learning experiences that unfold through PBL. Leverage students' communication skills by tapping them as community ambassadors for 21st century learning. For example, you might invite students to:

■ **Make presentations:** Students can make presentations about their school at feeder schools where younger students (and their parents) are considering their next steps. Younger students will appreciate the chance to hear from a "near peer" about the benefits and challenges of PBL.

■ **Share projects:** Look for opportunities for students to share their work with audiences who have an interest in 21st century learning, such as school boards, colleges of education, chambers of commerce, Rotary and other

> Establish ongoing relationships with nonprofit organizations, local businesses, or others that can benefit from students' 21st century competencies.

service clubs, or professional societies with an interest in building a pipeline of capable young people.

- **Offer student demonstrations:** Schools on the leading edge of 21st century learning have many requests from visitors who want to see this kind of learning in action. Have your students conduct PBL demonstrations at parent meetings or open houses. For example, they might walk parents through a day in the life of a PBL classroom or demonstrate how they use technology tools to collaborate. As an authentic project, have students produce brochures or videos that explain why learning looks the way it does in their classrooms. Share these on your school or district website. If your school is moving to PBL as a school-wide strategy, you might want to have students plan and conduct school tours. It's a good way for them to put their communications skills to work. (Schools in the High Tech High network and New Tech Network regularly offer student-led tours.)

4. Build system-wide support.

Although many courageous teachers have attempted to shift to PBL on their own, their efforts to accomplish 21st century learning goals can be challenging without school-wide support. It's difficult to be the only one in the building, for example, who assesses students on collaboration or communication as well as mastery of academic content. School leaders can help pave the way for PBL by creating policies and practices, such as those described below, that encourage a common culture of 21st century teaching and learning.

Updating Grading Systems for 21st Century Learning

Despite extended conversations about the importance of 21st century learning, few districts have yet taken the plunge of revising their report cards to include progress information about the 4 C's. That means most students and parents lack a clear picture of how students are developing in areas like collaboration and critical thinking. Although only a few pioneering districts and school networks have so far given traditional report cards a makeover, their experiences offer a preview of what's ahead for other school systems that are serious about developing students' 21st century competencies.

> Few districts have yet taken the plunge of revising their report cards to include progress information about the 4 C's.

"What You Assess Is What You Get"

The New Tech Network, which includes more than 100 PBL-based schools across the United States, takes a deliberate approach to teaching, assessing, and reporting on 21st century competencies. Napa New

Tech in California, first school in the network, set the stage by developing its skills-based grade book in 1998 (see example on the next page).

Paul Curtis, director of school quality for the network and previously a teacher at Napa New Tech, describes what made this new grading system revolutionary:

> *Instead of getting a "B-" on a research paper, a student would receive separate scores for categories like "content," "written communication," "critical thinking," and "work ethic." If the paper were turned in late, the work ethic score would drop but the others would remain the same. What was revolutionary about our grade book was that it totaled all of the "content" scores from all the different assignments and presented an overall assessment of the student's current level of content mastery. It would do the same for written communication, work ethic, collaboration, critical thinking, public speaking—basically, whatever skill categories the school put into the grade book. The system also allowed us to roll up those scores across classes and would produce an alternative progress report page that not only showed the course grades of a traditional progress report, but also showed how the student was scoring in the categories across classes.*

As the New Tech Network has evolved, it has continued to fine-tune its grading and reporting system and now uses a customized learning management system that makes grade books transparent for students and parents. What hasn't changed, Curtis says, is the emphasis on organizing assessment around both academic content and 21st century competencies. "What you assess is what you get," he adds.

Although competency-based report cards are new to most parents, it's not hard to convince them of the value of this updated system of communicating about student progress. "We can show parents a screenshot from a grade book and ask them, 'Where is this kid challenged?' In 10 seconds, they can spot areas where a student is weak, and right away we can talk about how we might help that student improve. Compared to traditional grade books," Curtis adds, "it's worlds apart."

Challenging a "Sacred Cow"

Schools in the Envision Learning Network, also PBL-based, have been on a similar path when it comes to designing an assessment and reporting system that reflects 21st century learning goals. "We started by asking, what do we want kids to know and be able to do? And how would we know they have achieved it?" explains Envision CEO Bob Lenz. Those questions have led to performance assessments and the use of portfolios to track student learning over time.

> Although competency-based report cards are new to most parents, it's not hard to convince them of the value of this system.

Algebra 2   1st Period (Semester 1) | John Kettleman

Edit Course Settings ▼

Term: Semester 1 ▼

| Start | Agendas | Projects | **Gradebook** | Discussions | Activities | Resources |

Class Stats

Enrolled Students
25

Students Below 70%
8

Grades Last Updated
11/22/2010

Content
72%

Professional Work Ethic
91%

Collaboration
84%

Written Communication
88%

Oral Communication
75%

Course Progress Reports for All Students

Students | Activities

Filter
Course Grades   ☑ All ☐ 100-90% ☐ 89-80% ☐ 79-70% ☐ 69-60% ☐ 59-0%

« Close

Period	Name▲	Grade	%	Content 70%	Professional Work Ethic 10%	Collaboration 10%	Written Communication 5%	Oral Communication 5%
1	Blair, Heidi	C-	70%	67%	91%	63%	*	92%
1	Borecky, James	C+	78%	73%	94%	91%	*	88%
1	Chan, Emily	A	93%	92%	98%	100%	90%	92%
1	Cooke-Smith, Tanisha	A-	92%	90%	99%	100%	85%	92%
1	Curry, Kevin	A-	92%	91%	97%	97%	*	92%
1	Davis, Tabitha	B-	82%	79%	89%	89%	90%	92%
1	Eads, William	C	73%	66%	89%	100%	*	88%

Source: newtechnetwork.org/echo

"We also asked, How should we structure schools (including assessment and reporting systems) to help do this work?"

Lenz acknowledges that changing grading systems means schools have to be willing "to take on a sacred cow." Teachers may have to give up their individual grading practices and adopt schoolwide rubrics that use common language to define quality work. As a staff, that means teachers need to come to agreement about what quality work looks like. "And that takes time," Lenz allows.

But the upside of reinventing grading systems is the benefit for students. "It's a gift for kids," Lenz says. "If you have common rubrics, they don't have to figure out the rules for six different teachers." Over the long term, having students use common rubrics to self-assess and reflect on their progress in specific areas helps them internalize learning goals, he adds.

Increasingly, Lenz hears from other schools and districts interested in taking assessment and reporting in a similar direction. He offers a few specific suggestions, based on 10 years' of effort to align 21st century instruction with performance-based assessment:

- **Emphasize professional development** so that teachers have shared conversations about updated grading and reporting practices.

- **Start with existing resources.** Rubrics for 21st century competencies have been developed by BIE, Envision, New Tech, and forward-looking districts such as Catalina Foothills in Arizona. "You don't have to write your own," Lenz says. "You make meaning by using a rubric, not by writing it. Mastery comes with implementation."

- **Examine student work and create exemplars.** Encourage your staff to examine and assess student work together. Do they have a common understanding of quality work? Over time, build a library of performance tasks that are aligned to common rubrics, Lenz suggests. For example, you might have a library of YouTube videos that show students making high-quality public presentations at the end of projects. (For more examples of archived student work, see the Envision Project Exchange at **envisionprojects.org**)

Systemic Support for 21st Century Learning

Providing system-wide support for 21st century learning doesn't have to mean additional work layered on top of other initiatives. Instead, consider how strategies to teach and assess the 4 C's fit within the context of efforts such as professional learning communities, curriculum mapping, and technology integration. Keep 21st century learning goals in mind when you are engaged in:

- **Curriculum mapping:** As you map the progression of learning goals from grade to grade, keep 21st century learning goals in mind. By incorporating goals for critical thinking, collaboration, communication, and creativity into curriculum maps, you reinforce the development of these key competencies over time.

- **Creating common assessment practices**: Adopt common language for assessing projects by creating shared rubrics, scoring guides, and work samples for assessing 21st century competencies. Such practices tell students that the 4 C's are important across the curriculum. Encourage teachers to share, discuss, and calibrate their assessments of student work samples.

> Encourage teachers to share, discuss, and calibrate their assessments of student work samples.

How to Communicate About 21st Century Learning with Parents and Other Stakeholders

At Da Vinci Charter Academy in Davis, California, students, faculty, and administrators all take an active role in sharing their story with the broader community. An all-PBL school that's part of the New Tech Network, Da Vinci serves about 300 students in grades 7-12. Listen to Principal Rody Boonchouy as he shares strategies that help to communicate the value of 21st century learning to future students, parents, and other community members:

▶ **Acculturating parents into a PBL program takes concerted effort** because we rely on parents as key partners in student-centered learning. At this point in our development, we have a reputation for a PBL pedagogy and collaborative dynamic. Many families are attracted to our school because of this, but the transition is still a significant paradigm shift.

▶ **Recruitment looks like this:** In the spring, student ambassadors design and lead presentations at local feeder schools (which are fantastic because these presentations truly are student designed). We invite parents to several parent-information nights where we provide an in-depth overview of the program, describe the whys and whats of PBL, and (most powerfully) invite current parents to give testimonials and speak about their experience to the visitors. Finally, we host shadowing days where prospective students come for half a day and are led by current students through activities to simulate PBL and let them get a feel for life on campus.

▶ **At the beginning of the year, we again host parent information nights** to educate families on logistics of PBL. This includes how to use our Learning Management System (to which they have full access to view projects, agendas, submitted assignments, and grade book), and to discuss how we go about grading. This piece is important because PBL is best assessed when explicit learning outcomes are taught and evaluated in a way that's aligned with our values. Our grade books disaggregate data for students' work ethic, collaboration, content, written communication, oral communication, and critical thinking.

▶ **Every year, we also hold a community meeting** for residents who live in proximity to the school. This is part of our effort to educate the community about the type of learning happening at Da Vinci. I provide an overview of the program and PBL, and we typically have a few student groups present recent projects as an example. Last year was powerful in that our Environmental Science course wrapped up a project on ways to "green" our campus and reduce our environmental footprint. These students presented at the community meeting, which initiated a broader discussion of how residents can partner with students at the school on green projects.

▶ **We are a highly public and transparent school.** We make an effort to be in the press as much as possible. Most major project presentations include an invite to our local reporter, who reliably covers PBL events.

- **Hiring new staff**: Ask teacher candidates how they plan to teach and assess 21st century competencies. Invite candidates to conduct a model 21st century lesson as part of their application process, or have them describe how they would remodel an existing project plan to emphasize one of the 4 C's. Ask them to describe how they make use of 21st century competencies and technology tools to deepen their professional practice.

- **Creating time for teacher collaboration**: If you want teachers to model collaboration, make sure they have time to work together. Encourage the use of critical friends protocols so that teachers benefit from peer feedback when they are designing projects (just as students benefit from feedback during projects). Have teachers share troubleshooting strategies to help overcome challenges during project implementation. Foster a culture of reflection by having colleagues debrief projects, discussing what worked well, what didn't, and what they might want to revise next time.

- **Eliminating barriers**: Find out what's getting in the way of successful development of 21st century competencies and work to eliminate barriers. This might mean reconsidering schedules, redistributing technology, or troubleshooting other challenges that can interfere with 21st century learning. Bring teachers into the problem-solving process, engaging their creativity and collaboration skills to generate practical solutions. For example, organizing volunteers to serve on presentation panels can be time-consuming for teachers. Consider recruiting a parent volunteer who serves as the point person for arranging visitors.

- **Connecting with community**: During the research phase of projects, students often need to connect with experts from outside school. Develop school-wide processes for connecting students with adult mentors and experts. Having an established network of experts available to consult will enable students to get the just-in-time help that they need to be successful.

Share Your Story

As your school or district develops resources and strategies for encouraging 21st century learning, look for opportunities to share your story with the broader education community. By presenting creative ideas at conferences, publishing your resources online, and collaborating with colleagues in other districts, you will be helping to disseminate good ideas. At the same time, you will be modeling effective use of the 21st century learning practices that you are encouraging in your students.

> Look for opportunities to share your story with the broader education community.

Afterword: Now It's Your Turn

In addition to teaching traditional content knowledge and skills, teachers can help students build competence in critical thinking, collaboration, communication, and creativity through well-designed Project Based Learning. We know this to be true, and the experiences of PBL teachers such as those profiled in the preceding pages shows it can be done. We hope this book has shown how to do it yourself, and that you feel confident and ready to "sail the 4 C's." Bon voyage!

More and more teachers and schools are gaining expertise in the use of PBL, so we think of this book as a work in progress. Some of you will have much to teach us in the coming years, and we'd like to hear from you. Stay in touch and send your questions, challenges and success stories to us at **bie.org**.

APPENDIX

Useful Stuff

About BIE Rubrics for 21st Century Competencies in PBL

What these rubrics assess

These rubrics describe what good critical thinking, collaboration, communication, and creativity and innovation look like in the context of Project Based Learning. The rubrics do not describe these competencies as they are seen generally or in other settings. For example, the Common Core State Standards for English/Language Arts call upon students to think critically when reading literature by making inferences and determining the author's intent. But since the *particular* content of projects will vary, the Critical Thinking Rubric for PBL only describes aspects of critical thinking that apply to tasks found in *all* projects, such as evaluating the reliability of a source of information. The same is true for communication; instead of describing competency in all types of communication, such as writing or listening to a speaker, we have chosen to focus the rubric on making a presentation, a competency common to all projects.

What these rubrics do NOT assess: "content"

These rubrics are designed to assess only the 4 C's, *not* subject-area knowledge in, say, math, history, or science. This content should be assessed with a separate rubric—or by adding rows to these rubrics. A "content + 4 C's" rubric can be created by the teacher for the particular product in the project, and target particular content standards. For example, the Presentation Rubric for PBL includes criteria for how well a student organizes ideas, speaks, and uses presentation aids. However, the rubric does not mention specific terminology, concepts, or subject-area information that should be used in the presentation, as determined by the teacher. The same goes for critical thinking; the rubric does not assess subject area knowledge when teams in a biology class decide if the government should fund gene therapy research or teams in an English class investigate the relevance of *Macbeth* to modern society. In other words, the rubric is designed to assess critical thinking skills used in projects anchored in subject-area content, but that content should be assessed separately.

How these rubrics align with Common Core State Standards

Competency in critical thinking, collaboration, communication, and creativity is required to meet many of the Common Core State Standards (CCSS) in English Language Arts and Literacy for History/Social Studies, Science, and Technical Subjects. The 4 C's are reflected in the "Mathematical Practices" section of CCSS, but not in the specific numbered standards, so they are not cited. In these rubrics, note that:

- Specific ELA standards are cited in the "At Standard" column only, but their intent is reflected in the "Approaching" and "Below" columns too.

- Exact CCSS language is used when possible—which could be useful as a vocabulary-building opportunity for students—but occasionally we used more student-friendly terms.

- The CCSS does not specifically address all of the 21st century competencies used in PBL, so some items appear on the rubrics without "CC" citations.

How to use these rubrics

The primary purpose of these rubrics is to help students reflect on their work and understand more clearly what they need to do to improve. Consider these tips for using the rubrics:

- Teachers may use the rubric as a source of guiding ideas for creating their own rubric, or choose not to use certain rows, or adapt the language to fit the needs of their students and the design of the project.

- Teachers should help students understand the rubric; give examples, explain new vocabulary words, put the language in their own words, and so on. Show models of the performance and have students practice using the rubric to assess them.

- Give students the rubric near the beginning of a project. Have them assess themselves and reflect on their progress at checkpoints and at the end.

- A student's performance may be described by some items in one column and some in another.

How to find evidence of 21st century competencies

Sources of evidence for 21st century competencies may include journals or other writing in which students document their use of the competency, self- and peer-reflections, and teacher observations. Another source of evidence is the product students create and/or their explanation of how it was created. For example, when students share project work with an audience a teacher can, in addition to assessing their competency in making a presentation, ask them to explain how they used critical thinking or followed the process of innovation.

How these rubrics are organized

Two of the rubrics, Critical Thinking and the "Process" section of Creativity and Innovation, are organized by the four phases of a typical project. This is because different aspects of these competencies come into play at different times. The other two rubrics, for Collaboration and Presentation, do not follow the phases of a project. The Presentation Rubric is only used in the last phase of a project, when students share their work with a public audience. However, competency in collaboration is relevant to *all* phases of a project. For example, a student should complete tasks on time, build on others' ideas, and show respect for teammates not just at the beginning of the project, but throughout it.

The columns along the top describe levels of quality:

1. *Below Standard*: What students do when they have not yet shown evidence of the competency.

2. *Approaching Standard*: What students do when they are showing some evidence of gaining the competency, but still have gaps or deficiencies.

3. *At Standard*: What students do when they show evidence of having gained the competency to an appropriate degree for their age and experience.

4. *Above Standard*: What students do when they go beyond what is expected to demonstrate competency. This column is left blank, with space for making a check mark. See the notes below on how to use this column.

How to use the "Above Standard" column

It's hard to predict or describe what a student may do when performing "Above Standard" but it's often the case that "you'll know it when you see it." For this reason, we've left this column blank. A teacher could wait until it happens, then describe it. For example, an advanced critical thinker might make an especially insightful analysis of a text or source of information. A student with advanced competency in collaboration might show leadership that brings out the talents and efforts of others on a team. A highly skilled presenter might use humor, emotion, stories, metaphors, or interactive features "like a pro." A creative product might have a "wow factor" or be similar to what an adult professional might create.

A teacher could also involve students in co-constructing language for the "Above Standard" column. Have them analyze samples of work from previous projects or professional products, then describe what makes them "go beyond expectations."

How to assign scores or grades

These rubrics do not feature a numerical scale—we leave it up to the teacher who uses them to decide how to assign scores or grades. Some dimensions may be given more or less weight. For example, on the Collaboration Rubric, "Helps the Team" might count for more than "Respects Others," depending on a teacher's goals.

Within each of the levels of quality described by the rubric, there could be variation, so a teacher may want to allow for a range of scores or points in each. For example, a *very* weak "Below Standard" performance could be scored a "1" and a "2" could indicate a *somewhat* weak performance. Similarly, a *very* advanced or "Above Standard" performance could be scored as a "6" with a "5" being "At Standard."

Feel free to draw language from the rubrics to create your own scoring guides for use with students, teachers, adult mentors, or presentation audience members.

(for grades 6-12; CCSS ELA aligned)

Critical Thinking Opportunity at Phases of a Project	Below Standard	Approaching Standard	At Standard	Above Standard ✓
Launching the Project: **Analyze Driving Question and Begin Inquiry**	▸ sees only superficial aspects of, or one point of view on, the Driving Question	▸ identifies some central aspects of the Driving Question, but may not see complexities or consider various points of view ▸ asks some follow-up questions about the topic or the wants and needs of the audience or users of a product, but does not dig deep	▸ shows understanding of central aspects of the Driving Question by identifying in detail what needs to be known to answer it and considering various possible points of view on it ▸ asks follow-up questions that focus or broaden inquiry, as appropriate (CC 6-12.W.7) ▸ asks follow-up questions to gain understanding of the wants and needs of audience or product users	
Building Knowledge, Understanding, and Skills: **Gather and Evaluate Information**	▸ is unable to integrate information to address the Driving Question; gathers too little, too much, or irrelevant information, or from too few sources ▸ accepts information at face value (does not evaluate its quality)	▸ attempts to integrate information to address the Driving Question, but it may be too little, too much, or gathered from too few sources; some of it may not be relevant ▸ understands that the quality of information should be considered, but does not do so thoroughly	▸ integrates relevant and sufficient information to address the Driving Question, gathered from multiple and varied sources (CC 6,11-12.RI.7) ▸ thoroughly assesses the quality of information (considers usefulness, accuracy and credibility; distinguishes fact vs. opinion; recognizes bias) (CC 6-12.W.8)	
Developing and Revising Ideas and Products: **Use Evidence and Criteria**	▸ accepts arguments for possible answers to the Driving Question without questioning whether reasoning is valid ▸ uses evidence without considering how strong it is ▸ relies on "gut feeling" to evaluate and revise ideas, product prototypes or problem solutions (does not use criteria)	▸ recognizes the need for valid reasoning and strong evidence, but does not evaluate it carefully when developing answers to the Driving Question ▸ evaluates and revises ideas, product prototypes or problem solutions based on incomplete or invalid criteria	▸ evaluates arguments for possible answers to the Driving Question by assessing whether reasoning is valid and evidence is relevant and sufficient (CC 6-12.SL.3, RI.8) ▸ justifies choice of criteria used to evaluate ideas, product prototypes or problem solutions ▸ revises inadequate drafts, designs or solutions and explains why they will better meet evaluation criteria (CC 6-12.W.5)	
Presenting Products and Answers to Driving Question: **Justify Choices, Consider Alternatives & Implications**	▸ chooses one presentation medium without considering advantages and disadvantages of using other mediums to present a particular topic or idea ▸ cannot give valid reasons or supporting evidence to defend choices made when answering the Driving Question or creating products ▸ does not consider alternative answers to the Driving Question, designs for products, or points of view ▸ is not able to explain important new understanding gained in the project	▸ considers the advantages and disadvantages of using different mediums to present a particular topic or idea, but not thoroughly ▸ explains choices made when answering the Driving Question or creating products, but some reasons are not valid or lack supporting evidence ▸ understands that there may be alternative answers to the Driving Question or designs for products, but does not consider them carefully ▸ can explain some things learned in the project, but is not entirely clear about new understanding	▸ evaluates the advantages and disadvantages of using different mediums to present a particular topic or idea (CC 8.RI.7) ▸ justifies choices made when answering the Driving Question or creating products, by giving valid reasons with supporting evidence (CC 6-12.SL.4) ▸ recognizes the limitations of an answer to the Driving Question or a product design (how it might not be complete, certain, or perfect) and considers alternative perspectives (CC 11-12.SL.4) ▸ can clearly explain new understanding gained in the project and how it might transfer to other situations or contexts	

COLLABORATION RUBRIC for PBL

(for grades 6-12; CCSS ELA aligned)

Individual Performance	Below Standard	Approaching Standard	At Standard	Above Standard ✔
Takes Responsibility for Oneself	▸ is not prepared, informed, and ready to work with the team ▸ does not use technology tools as agreed upon by the team to communicate and manage project tasks ▸ does not do project tasks ▸ does not complete tasks on time ▸ does not use feedback from others to improve work	▸ is usually prepared, informed, and ready to work with the team ▸ uses technology tools as agreed upon by the team to communicate and manage project tasks, but not consistently ▸ does some project tasks, but needs to be reminded ▸ completes most tasks on time ▸ sometimes uses feedback from others to improve work	▸ is prepared and ready to work; is well informed on the project topic and cites evidence to probe and reflect on ideas with the team (CC 6-12.SL.1a) ▸ consistently uses technology tools as agreed upon by the team to communicate and manage project tasks ▸ does tasks without having to be reminded ▸ completes tasks on time ▸ uses feedback from others to improve work	
Helps the Team	▸ does not help the team solve problems; may cause problems ▸ does not ask probing questions, express ideas, or elaborate in response to questions in discussions ▸ does not give useful feedback to others ▸ does not offer to help others if they need it	▸ cooperates with the team but may not actively help it solve problems ▸ sometimes expresses ideas clearly, asks probing questions, and elaborates in response to questions in discussions ▸ gives feedback to others, but it may not always be useful ▸ sometimes offers to help others if they need it	▸ helps the team solve problems and manage conflicts ▸ makes discussions effective by clearly expressing ideas, asking probing questions, making sure everyone is heard, responding thoughtfully to new information and perspectives (CC 6-12.SL.1c) ▸ gives useful feedback (specific, feasible, supportive) to others so they can improve their work ▸ offers to help others do their work if needed	
Respects Others	▸ is impolite or unkind to teammates (may interrupt, ignore ideas, hurt feelings) ▸ does not acknowledge or respect other perspectives	▸ is usually polite and kind to teammates ▸ usually acknowledges and respects other perspectives and disagrees diplomatically	▸ is polite and kind to teammates ▸ acknowledges and respects other perspectives; disagrees diplomatically	

Team Performance	Below Standard	Approaching Standard	At Standard	Above Standard ✔
Makes and Follows Agreements	▸ does not discuss how the team will work together ▸ does not follow rules for collegial discussions, decision-making and conflict resolution ▸ does not discuss how well agreements are being followed ▸ allows breakdowns in team work to happen; needs teacher to intervene	▸ discusses how the team will work together, but not in detail; may just "go through the motions" when creating an agreement ▸ usually follows rules for collegial discussions, decision-making, and conflict resolution ▸ discusses how well agreements are being followed, but not in depth; may ignore subtle issues ▸ notices when norms are not being followed but asks the teacher for help to resolve issues	▸ makes detailed agreements about how the team will work together, including the use of technology tools ▸ follows rules for collegial discussions (CC 6-12.SL.1b), decision-making, and conflict resolution ▸ honestly and accurately discusses how well agreements are being followed ▸ takes appropriate action when norms are not being followed; attempts to resolve issues without asking the teacher for help	
Organizes Work	▸ does project work without creating a task list ▸ does not set a schedule and track progress toward goals and deadlines ▸ does not assign roles or share leadership; one person may do too much, or all members may do random tasks ▸ wastes time and does not run meetings well; materials, drafts, notes are not organized (may be misplaced or inaccessible)	▸ creates a task list that divides project work among the team, but it may not be in detail or followed closely ▸ sets a schedule for doing tasks but does not follow it closely ▸ assigns roles but does not follow them, or selects only one "leader" who makes most decisions ▸ usually uses time and runs meetings well, but may occasionally waste time; keeps materials, drafts, notes, but not always organized	▸ creates a detailed task list that divides project work reasonably among the team (CC 6-12.SL.1b) ▸ sets a schedule and tracks progress toward goals and deadlines (CC 6-12.SL.1b) ▸ assigns roles if and as needed, based on team members' strengths (CC 6-12.SL.1b) ▸ uses time and runs meetings efficiently; keeps materials, drafts, notes organized	
Works as a Whole Team	▸ does not recognize or use special talents of team members ▸ does project tasks separately and does not put them together; it is a collection of individual work	▸ makes some attempt to use special talents of team members ▸ does most project tasks separately and puts them together at the end	▸ recognizes and uses special talents of each team member ▸ develops ideas and creates products with involvement of all team members; tasks done separately are brought to the team for critique and revision	

PRESENTATION RUBRIC for PBL

(for grades 6–8; Common Core ELA aligned)

	Below Standard	Approaching Standard	At Standard	Above Standard ✔
Explanation of Ideas & Information	▸ uses too few, inappropriate, or irrelevant descriptions, facts, details, or examples to support ideas	▸ uses some descriptions, facts, details, and examples that support ideas, but there may not be enough, or some are irrelevant	▸ uses relevant, well-chosen descriptions, facts, details, and examples to support claims, findings, arguments, or an answer to a Driving Question (CC 6-8.SL.4)	
Organization	▸ does not include important parts required in the presentation ▸ does not have a main idea or presents ideas in an order that does not make sense ▸ does not have an introduction and/or conclusion ▸ uses time poorly; the whole presentation, or a part of it, is too short or too long	▸ includes almost everything required in the presentation ▸ moves from one idea to the next, but main idea may not be clear or some ideas may be in the wrong order ▸ has an introduction and conclusion, but they are not effective ▸ generally times presentation well, but may spend too much or too little time on a topic, a/v aid, or idea	▸ includes everything required in the presentation ▸ states main idea and moves from one idea to the next in a logical order, emphasizing main points in a focused, coherent manner (CC 6-8.SL.4) ▸ has an effective introduction and conclusion ▸ organizes time well; no part of the presentation is rushed, too short or too long	
Eyes & Body	▸ does not look at audience; reads notes or slides ▸ does not use gestures or movements ▸ lacks poise and confidence (fidgets, slouches, appears nervous) ▸ wears clothing inappropriate for the occasion	▸ makes infrequent eye contact; reads notes or slides most of the time ▸ uses a few gestures or movements but they do not look natural ▸ shows some poise and confidence (only a little fidgeting or nervous movement) ▸ makes some attempt to wear clothing appropriate for the occasion	▸ keeps eye contact with audience most of the time; only glances at notes or slides (CC 6-8.SL.4) ▸ uses natural gestures and movements ▸ looks poised and confident ▸ wears clothing appropriate for the occasion	
Voice	▸ mumbles or speaks too quickly or slowly ▸ speaks too softly to be understood ▸ frequently uses "filler" words ("uh, um, so, and, like, etc.") ▸ does not speak appropriately for the context and task (may be too informal, use slang)	▸ speaks clearly most of the time; sometimes too quickly or slowly ▸ speaks loudly enough for most of the audience to hear, but may speak in a monotone ▸ occasionally uses filler words ▸ tries to speak appropriately for the context and task	▸ speaks clearly; not too quickly or slowly (CC 6-8.SL.4) ▸ speaks loudly enough for everyone to hear; changes tone to maintain interest (CC 6-8.SL.4) ▸ rarely uses filler words ▸ speaks appropriately for the context and task, demonstrating command of formal English when appropriate (CC 6-8.SL.6)	

	Below Standard	Approaching Standard	At Standard	Above Standard ✔
Presentation Aids	▸ does not use audio/visual aids or media ▸ attempts to use one or a few audio/visual aids or media but they distract from or do not add to the presentation	▸ uses audio/visual aids or media, but they sometimes distract from or do not add to the presentation	▸ uses well-produced audio/visual aids or media to clarify information, emphasize important points, strengthen arguments, and add interest (CC 6-8.SL.5)	
Response to Audience Questions	▸ does not address audience questions (goes off topic or misunderstands without seeking clarification)	▸ answers some audience questions, but not always clearly or completely	▸ answers audience questions clearly and completely ▸ seeks clarification, admits "I don't know," or explains how the answer might be found when unable to answer a question	
Participation in Team Presentations	▸ Not all team members participate; only one or two speak	▸ All team members participate, but not equally	▸ All team members participate for about the same length of time ▸ All team members are able to answer questions about the topic as a whole, not just their part of it	

PRESENTATION RUBRIC for PBL

(for grades 9–12; Common Core ELA aligned)

	Below Standard	Approaching Standard	At Standard	Above Standard ✔
Explanation of Ideas & Information	▸ does not present information, arguments, ideas, or findings clearly, concisely, and logically; argument lacks supporting evidence; audience cannot follow the line of reasoning ▸ selects information, develops ideas and uses a style inappropriate to the purpose, task, and audience (may be too much or too little information, or the wrong approach) ▸ does not address alternative or opposing perspectives	▸ presents information, findings, arguments and supporting evidence in a way that is not always clear, concise, and logical; line of reasoning is sometimes hard to follow ▸ attempts to select information, develop ideas and use a style appropriate to the purpose, task, and audience but does not fully succeed ▸ attempts to address alternative or opposing perspectives, but not clearly or completely	▸ presents information, findings, arguments and supporting evidence clearly, concisely, and logically; audience can easily follow the line of reasoning (CC 9-12.SL.4) ▸ selects information, develops ideas and uses a style appropriate to the purpose, task, and audience (CC 9-12.SL.4) ▸ clearly and completely addresses alternative or opposing perspectives (CC 11-12.SL.4)	
Organization	▸ does not meet requirements for what should be included in the presentation ▸ does not have an introduction and/or conclusion ▸ uses time poorly; the whole presentation, or a part of it, is too short or too long	▸ meets most requirements for what should be included in the presentation ▸ has an introduction and conclusion, but they are not clear or interesting ▸ generally times presentation well, but may spend too much or too little time on a topic, a/v aid, or idea	▸ meets all requirements for what should be included in the presentation ▸ has a clear and interesting introduction and conclusion ▸ organizes time well; no part of the presentation is too short or too long	
Eyes & Body	▸ does not look at audience; reads notes or slides ▸ does not use gestures or movements ▸ lacks poise and confidence (fidgets, slouches, appears nervous) ▸ wears clothing inappropriate for the occasion	▸ makes infrequent eye contact; reads notes or slides most of the time ▸ uses a few gestures or movements but they do not look natural ▸ shows some poise and confidence, (only a little fidgeting or nervous movement) ▸ makes some attempt to wear clothing appropriate for the occasion	▸ keeps eye contact with audience most of the time; only glances at notes or slides ▸ uses natural gestures and movements ▸ looks poised and confident ▸ wears clothing appropriate for the occasion	
Voice	▸ mumbles or speaks too quickly or slowly ▸ speaks too softly to be understood ▸ frequently uses "filler" words ("uh, um, so, and, like, etc.") ▸ does not adapt speech for the context and task	▸ speaks clearly most of the time ▸ speaks loudly enough for the audience to hear most of the time, but may speak in a monotone ▸ occasionally uses filler words ▸ attempts to adapt speech for the context and task but is unsuccessful or inconsistent	▸ speaks clearly; not too quickly or slowly ▸ speaks loudly enough for everyone to hear; changes tone and pace to maintain interest ▸ rarely uses filler words ▸ adapts speech for the context and task, demonstrating command of formal English when appropriate (CC 9-12.SL.6)	

	Below Standard	Approaching Standard	At Standard	Above Standard ✔
Presentation Aids	▸ does not use audio/visual aids or media ▸ attempts to use one or a few audio/visual aids or media, but they do not add to or may distract from the presentation	▸ uses audio/visual aids or media, but they may sometimes distract from or not add to the presentation ▸ sometimes has trouble bringing audio/visual aids or media smoothly into the presentation	▸ uses well-produced audio/visual aids or media to enhance understanding of findings, reasoning, and evidence, and to add interest (CC 9-12.SL.5) ▸ smoothly brings audio/visual aids or media into the presentation	
Response to Audience Questions	▸ does not address audience questions (goes off topic or misunderstands without seeking clarification)	▸ answers audience questions, but not always clearly or completely	▸ answers audience questions clearly and completely ▸ seeks clarification, admits "I don't know" or explains how the answer might be found when unable to answer a question	
Participation in Team Presentations	▸ Not all team members participate; only one or two speak	▸ All team members participate, but not equally	▸ All team members participate for about the same length of time ▸ All team members are able to answer questions about the topic as a whole, not just their part of it	

CREATIVITY & INNOVATION RUBRIC for PBL

(for grades 6-12; CCSS ELA aligned)

PROCESS

Creativity & Innovation Opportunity at Phases of a Project	Below Standard	Approaching Standard	At Standard	Above Standard ✓
Launching the Project **Define the Creative Challenge**	▸ may just "follow directions" without understanding the purpose for innovation or considering the needs and interests of the target audience	▸ understands the basic purpose for innovation but does not thoroughly consider the needs and interests of the target audience	▸ understands the purpose driving the process of innovation (Who needs this? Why?) ▸ develops insight about the particular needs and interests of the target audience	
Building Knowledge, Understanding, and Skills **Identify Sources of Information**	▸ uses only typical sources of information (website, book, article) ▸ does not offer new ideas during discussions	▸ finds one or two sources of information that are not typical ▸ offers new ideas during discussions, but stays within narrow perspectives	▸ in addition to typical sources, finds unusual ways or places to get information (adult expert, community member, business or organization, literature) ▸ promotes divergent and creative perspectives during discussions (CC 11-12.SL.1c)	
Developing and Revising Ideas and Products **Generate and Select Ideas**	▸ stays within existing frameworks; does not use idea-generating techniques to develop new ideas for product(s) ▸ selects one idea without evaluating the quality of ideas ▸ does not ask new questions or elaborate on the selected idea ▸ reproduces existing ideas; does not imagine new ones ▸ does not consider or use feedback and critique to revise product	▸ develops some original ideas for product(s), but could develop more with better use of idea-generating techniques ▸ evaluates ideas, but not thoroughly before selecting one ▸ asks a few new questions but may make only minor changes to the selected idea ▸ shows some imagination when shaping ideas into a product, but may stay within conventional boundaries ▸ considers and may use some feedback and critique to revise a product, but does not seek it out	▸ uses idea-generating techniques to develop several original ideas for product(s) ▸ carefully evaluates the quality of ideas and selects the best one to shape into a product ▸ asks new questions, takes different perspectives to elaborate and improve on the selected idea ▸ uses ingenuity and imagination, going outside conventional boundaries, when shaping ideas into a product ▸ seeks out and uses feedback and critique to revise product to better meet the needs of the intended audience (CC 6-12.W.5)	
Presenting Products and Answers to Driving Question **Present Work to Users/Target Audience**	▸ presents ideas and products in typical ways (text-heavy PowerPoint slides, recitation of notes, no interactive features)	▸ adds some interesting touches to presentation media ▸ attempts to include elements in presentation that make it more lively and engaging	▸ creates visually exciting presentation media ▸ includes elements in presentation that are especially fun, lively, engaging, or powerful to the particular audience	

PRODUCT

	Below Standard	Approaching Standard	At Standard	Above Standard ✔
Originality	▸ relies on existing models, ideas, or directions; it is not new or unique ▸ follows rules and conventions; uses materials and ideas in typical ways	▸ has some new ideas or improvements, but some ideas are predictable or conventional ▸ may show a tentative attempt to step outside rules and conventions, or find new uses for common materials or ideas	▸ is new, unique, surprising; shows a personal touch ▸ may successfully break rules and conventions, or use common materials or ideas in new, clever and surprising ways	
Value	▸ is not useful or valuable to the intended audience/user ▸ would not work in the real world; impractical or unfeasible	▸ is useful and valuable to some extent; it may not solve certain aspects of the defined problem or exactly meet the identified need ▸ unclear if product would be practical or feasible	▸ is seen as useful and valuable; it solves the defined problem or meets the identified need ▸ is practical, feasible	
Style	▸ is safe, ordinary, made in a conventional style ▸ has several elements that do not fit together; it is a mish-mash	▸ has some interesting touches, but lacks a distinct style ▸ has some elements that may be excessive or do not fit together well	▸ is well-crafted, striking, designed with a distinct style but still appropriate for the purpose ▸ combines different elements into a coherent whole	

Note: The term "product" is used in this rubric as an umbrella term for the result of the process of innovation during a project. A product may be a constructed object, proposal, presentation, solution to a problem, service, system, work of art or piece of writing, an invention, event, an improvement to an existing product, etc.

PROJECT AUDIENCE FEEDBACK: 4C's

Student Name/Team:	

Project Name:		Date:	

Thank you for taking the time to answer the following questions:

1. What evidence did you see that students showed competence in critical thinking?

2. What evidence did you see that students showed competence in collaboration?

3. What evidence did you see that students showed competence in communication?

4. What evidence did you see that students showed competence in creativity and innovation?

Student Reflection Prompts for the 4 C's

Reflection is an essential element of every project. By encouraging students to reflect on the 4 C's, you will prompt them to think about the progress they're making in developing these important 21st century competencies.

Vary reflection activities to keep things fresh for students. Early in the project, for example, you might have students capture their reflections in writing (in a project journal or on a blog). This will generate artifacts they can review later, encouraging more rounds of reflection. Mid-project, you might switch it up and have students reflect aloud — during a team meeting, one-on-one with a partner, as a whole-class activity, in a fishbowl, or as a podcast. At the end of the project, incorporate reflection into culminating events and make sure it's part of final assessment. For example, consider having students explain to their parents (in writing or at a conference) why they received the grades they did for collaboration, communication, creativity, or critical thinking.

Here are suggested reflection prompts to encourage deeper thinking about each "C."

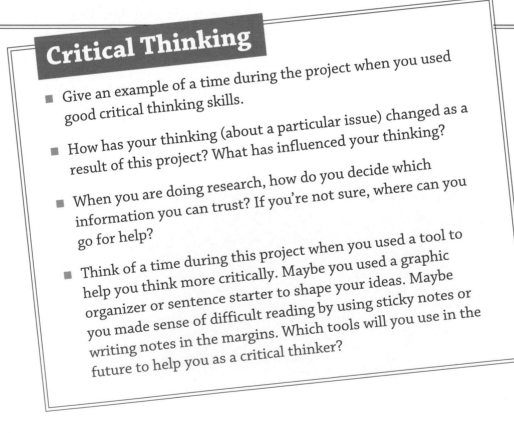

Critical Thinking

- Give an example of a time during the project when you used good critical thinking skills.

- How has your thinking (about a particular issue) changed as a result of this project? What has influenced your thinking?

- When you are doing research, how do you decide which information you can trust? If you're not sure, where can you go for help?

- Think of a time during this project when you used a tool to help you think more critically. Maybe you used a graphic organizer or sentence starter to shape your ideas. Maybe you made sense of difficult reading by using sticky notes or writing notes in the margins. Which tools will you use in the future to help you as a critical thinker?

Collaboration

- Make a prediction (at the start of a project): Why do you think collaboration is going to be essential for your team's success?

- How are you making sure your team takes advantage of everyone's talents (including yours)?

- Describe a collaboration challenge your team has faced (such as trouble coming to consensus). How did you attempt to resolve it? What happened? What else could you try?

- What have you learned about teamwork that will help in your next project?

Communication

- Describe how you feel about your upcoming presentation (or interview with an expert). If you have the jitters, what can you do to feel better prepared and less anxious?

- At your public presentation, how did the audience respond? Describe one thing you did that you think helped to engage your audience.

- How has your understanding of being a good listener changed during this project? Why?

- What do you want to get better at when it comes to communication?

Creativity

- Describe a time during this project when you took a creative risk. What did that feel like? What happened as a result?

- What's something you've learned about creative thinkers that surprised you? Why?

- What are some problems you had to solve during the project? How did you solve the problems?

- Think about something that you or your team tried during this project that didn't work very well. How did you respond? What did you do next?

Frequently Asked Questions about PBL and 21st Century Learning

What is Project Based Learning and how does it prepare students for 21st century challenges?

PBL is a teaching method that uses "projects" to organize the curriculum. Students learn important academic content through well-designed projects by investigating questions, generating and evaluating solutions, and producing products that demonstrate what they have learned. At the same time, students deepen their ability to think critically, collaborate, communicate, and solve problems creatively. They also get better at directing their own learning, managing their time, and working with diverse team members on shared goals. These competencies are all considered essential preparation for college and careers.

How can we make sure students are getting 21st century benefits from PBL?

The short answer is to do rigorous Project Based Learning rather than simply "doing projects." PBL incorporates essential features that aren't necessarily present in the projects many of us may have seen in the past or done when we were students. The Buck Institute for Education (**bie.org**) explains the difference this way: In well-designed PBL, projects are the "main course" of learning. They aren't tacked on at the end of a unit as "dessert."

What's more, in PBL, a well-designed project:

- **is organized around an open-ended Driving Question or challenge.** Authentic and significant questions, issues, and/or problems focus students' work and deepen their learning. Inquiry-based learning encourages curiosity as a habit of mind.

- **creates a need to know essential content and develop 21st century competencies.** PBL begins with the vision of an end product or presentation which requires students to acquire specific knowledge, understand concepts, and employ strategies such as collaboration and creative problem solving. This gives students a context for their work, a reason to learn, and motivation to develop and apply 21st century competencies.

- **requires inquiry to learn and/or create something new.** PBL requires students to construct something new — an idea, a solution, an interpretation, a new way of displaying what they have learned.

- **results in a publicly presented product or performance.** Students need to demonstrate what they have learned by showing and explaining their work to others for scrutiny and critique. Presenting to an audience not only adds motivation and increases engagement, but causes students to practice effective communication. That's another important 21st century competency.

- **allows some degree of student voice and choice.** In PBL, students learn to work independently and take responsibility when they are asked to make choices. The opportunity to make choices, and to express their learning in their own voice, also helps increase student engagement in their education. In today's dynamic world, self-directed learners are better able to adapt to rapid change.

- **requires critical thinking, problem solving, collaboration, and various forms of communication.** To answer the Driving Question and produce high-quality work, students need to do much more than remember information. They need to think deeply and critically about what and how they are learning. PBL provides opportunities for students to learn how to work together in a team effort, solve problems creatively, use technology tools, and explain their work to an audience. Through successive project experiences, students move toward mastery of these important competencies.

How does PBL prepare students for college?

Students can have difficulty in college if they haven't learned to problem-solve and take responsibility for their own learning. PBL provides students with a shepherded practice run, where they have to make decisions, monitor their progress, work with other students, manage time and resources, and communicate what they have learned. PBL teachers provide essential support so that students can "grow into" these competencies. Nothing can guarantee college success, but PBL provides more opportunities than traditional instruction for students to develop the self-management skills they will need to succeed in college, as well as future careers.

How does PBL encourage career readiness?

The competencies that students develop through projects — knowing how to work with others, understand diverse perspectives, think critically, reach consensus, and communicate effectively — will be assets in any career. Because projects often involve research beyond the classroom, students also gain opportunities to connect with and learn from experts and role models from a variety of career fields.

What does research tell us about PBL and 21st century skills?

When it comes to helping students understand important academic content, research shows that PBL, when done well, is at least as effective as traditional instructional approaches, and there are many studies that show PBL to be superior. Specifically, PBL-type instruction has been shown to:

- increase understanding of concepts and the ability to apply knowledge as measured by standardized tests of subject matter
- enable students to remember what they have learned and use that knowledge in new situations
- enable students to learn how to work in groups, solve problems, and communicate what they have learned

PBL also has a strong track record when it comes to promoting student engagement among diverse learners. That's understandable, because projects give students a greater voice in their own learning. PBL encourages a need to know important content along with a need to develop the competencies required to accomplish authentic work.

Will PBL take too much time away from learning traditional subject matter in favor of building non-content-related skills?

When done right, PBL emphasizes important academic learning goals *and* 21st century competencies. It's not an either/or proposition. As students become more effective communicators and collaborators, better critical thinkers, and more confident about proposing creative solutions, they are able to go deeper with investigations of important content. If you need convincing, make time to attend a project showcase. Be an active audience member. Ask questions of students who are presenting their work and listen for evidence of deep learning.

Research Summary:
PBL and 21st Century Competencies

Project Based Learning has been shown to yield a number of benefits for students, ranging from deeper learning of academic content to stronger motivation to learn. Looking specifically at how PBL supports 21st century learning goals, we can find several promising areas, including:

Academic achievement:

Goals for 21st century learning emphasize mastery of significant academic content, which also is the foundation of any well-designed project. Comparisons of learning outcomes in PBL versus more traditional, textbook-and-lecture driven instruction show that:

- Students learning through PBL retain content longer and have a deeper understanding of what they are learning.
  (Penuel & Means, 2000; Stepien, Gallagher & Workman, 1993)

- In specific content areas, PBL has been shown to be more effective than traditional methods for teaching math, economics, language, science, and other disciplines.
  (Beckett & Miller, 2006; Boaler, 2002; Finkelstein et al., 2010; Greier et al., 2008; Mergendoller, Maxwell, & Bellisimo, 2006)

- On high-stakes tests, PBL students perform as well or better than traditionally taught students.
  (Parker et al., 2011)

21st century competencies:

PBL helps students master the key competencies identified as essential for college and career readiness. Research has shown:

- Students demonstrate better problem-solving skills in PBL than in more traditional classes and are able to apply what they learn to real-life situations.
  (Finkelstein et al., 2010)

- When teachers are trained in PBL methods, they devote more class time to teaching 21st century skills; their students perform at least as well on standardized tests as students engaged in traditional instruction.
  (Hixson, Ravitz, & Whisman, 2012)

- PBL students also show improved critical thinking.
  (Beckett & Miller, 2006; Horan, Lavaroni, & Beldon, 1996; Mergendoller, Maxwell, & Bellisimo, 2006; Tretten & Zachariou, 1995)

- Through PBL experiences, students improve their ability to work collaboratively and resolve conflicts.
  (Beckett & Miller; ChanLin, 2008)

- Opportunities for collaborative learning provide benefits to students across grade levels, academic subjects, and achievement levels.
  (Johnson & Johnson, 2009; Slavin, 1996)

Equity:

- PBL shows promise as a strategy for closing the achievement gap by engaging lower-achieving students.
  (Boaler, 2002; Penuel & Means, 2000)

- PBL can work in different types of schools, serving diverse learners.
  (Hixson, Ravitz, & Whisman, 2012)

- PBL also can provide an effective model for whole-school reform.
  (National Clearinghouse for Comprehensive School Reform, 2004; Newmann & Wehlage, 1995; Ravitz, 2008)

Motivation:

- In PBL classrooms, students demonstrate improved attitudes toward learning. They exhibit more engagement, are more self-reliant, and have better attendance than in more traditional settings.
  (Thomas, 2000; Walker & Leary, 2009)

Teacher satisfaction:

- Teachers may need time and professional development to become familiar with PBL methods, but those who make this shift in classroom practice report increased job satisfaction.
  (Hixson, Ravitz, & Whisman, 2012; Strobel & van Barneveld, 2009)

For links to full text of studies as well as updates on research about Project Based Learning, visit the Buck Institute for Education at **bie.org.**

Recommended Readings and Helpful Resources

21st Century Learning

Recommended Readings

- *21st Century Skills: Rethinking How Students Learn,* edited by James Bellanca and Ron Brandt, includes essays from leading thinkers about new demands on students, teachers, and school leaders in the era of rapid change.

- *The Leader's Guide to 21st Century Education,* by Ken Kay and Valerie Greenhill, outlines a seven-step process to help schools better prepare students for 21st century challenges.

- *Teaching the iGeneration: 5 Easy Ways to Introduce Essential Skills with Web 2.0 Tools,* by William Ferriter and Adam Garry, combines technology integration strategies with practical observations for the 21st century classroom, such as how to tell powerful visual stories and how to make conversations safe for all learners.

Helpful Resources

- Edutopia (**edutopia.org**) offers a wealth of videos and resources that show 21st century learning in action. For example, detailed case studies in the Schools That Work series illustrate how to encourage collaborative learning and critical thinking.

- International Society for Technology in Education, or ISTE, publishes the National Educational Technology Standards (**iste.org**).

- Partnership for 21st Century Skills, known as P21 (**p21.org**) provides extensive resources about defining and implementing the 4 C's.

4 C's

Recommended Readings

- *Bringing Innovation to School: Empowering Learners to Thrive in a Changing World,* by Suzie Boss, offers examples of schools that are moving ahead on the innovation front and introduces strategies to encourage students to become more innovative thinkers and doers.

- *Creating Innovators: The Making of Young People Who Will Change the World,* by Tony Wagner, describes how successful young adults have developed their innovative mindset and suggests how schools must change to foster more innovation.

- *Thinking Through Quality Questioning: Deepening Student Engagement,* by Jackie Walsh and Beth Sattes, provides a framework of teacher behaviors that are linked to better student thinking. The authors focus on how to build a collaborative classroom culture and create norms for questioning and thinking.

- *Out of Our Minds: Learning to Be Creative,* by Sir Ken Robinson, explores why many people think they are not creative and offers solutions — including suggestions for education — to reconnect us with the creative impulse.

- *Well Spoken: Teaching Speaking to All Students,* by Erik Palmer, explains how and why to teach speaking skills across the curriculum so that students become more effective, and confident, communicators.

- *World Class Learners: Educating Creative and Entrepreneurial Students*, by Yong Zhao, takes a global look at education trends and explains, with research-backed arguments, why students need to develop a more entrepreneurial mindset.

Helpful Resources

- The Center for Critical Thinking and Moral Critique and Foundation for Critical Thinking (**criticalthinking.org**) are sister nonprofit organizations that work closely to promote educational reform. They offer workshops, conferences, research, professional development, and other resources to cultivate critical thinking.

- The Critical Thinking Consortium (**tc2.ca**), based in Canada, supports the infusion of critical thinking across all subject areas through curriculum development, professional development, research, and resource sharing.

- National Center for Teaching Thinking (**nctt.net**) provides professional development and resources to encourage the teaching and assessing of skillful thinking, from K-12 through college.

- On Innovation (**oninnovation.com**), a project of the Henry Ford Museum, offers an online library of interviews with innovators past and present.

- Stanford d.school (**dschool.stanford.edu**), formally known as the Hasso Plattner Institute of Design at Stanford, is a hub for fostering innovative thinking through the design process. Resources for K-12 educators include a d.school Boot Camp and K-12 wiki.

Common Core

Recommended Readings

- *Pathways to the Common Core: Accelerating Achievement*, by Lucy Calkins, Mary Ehrenworth, and Christopher Lehman, provides guidance to help students meet the Common Core standards in literacy. Along the way, the authors debunk Common Core myths and put the responsibility for interpreting and implementing the standards on the shoulders of teachers and school leaders.

- *Teaching Students to Read Like Detectives: Comprehending, Analyzing, and Discussing Text*, by Douglas Fisher, Nancy Frey, and Diane Lapp, offers strategies to help students engage with difficult text and meet the higher literacy expectations of the Common Core.

English Learners

Recommended Readings

- *The ESL/ELL Teacher's Survival Guide: Ready-to-Use Strategies, Tools, and Activities for Teaching English Language Learners of All Levels*, by Larry Ferlazzo and Katie Hull Sypnieski, offers classroom-tested strategies for meeting the needs of English learner students.

- *Sheltered Content Instruction: Teaching English Language Learners with Diverse Abilities (4th Edition)*, by Jana J. Echevarria and Anne Graves, offers a systematic approach for assessing and meeting the needs of the diverse and growing number of students who are English learners.

References

- Arnold, A. (n.d.). Creative product semantic scale. *Product Enthusiast* (blog). **http://alicarnold.wordpress.com/cpss**

- Aspen Institute. (2008). *Youth entrepreneurship education in America: A policymaker's action guide*. Washington, DC: Author.

- Boaler, J. (2002). Learning from teaching: Exploring the relationship between reform curriculum and equity. *Journal for Research in Mathematics Education, 33*(4), 239-258. Retrieved from **http://tnl.esd113.org/cms/lib3/WA01001093/Centricity/ModuleInstance/276/BoalerReformCurriculumandequity.pdf**

- Boss, S. (2012). *Bringing innovation to school: Empowering students to thrive in a changing world*. Bloomington, IN: Solution Tree.

- Bronson, P., & Merryman, A. (2010, July 10). The creativity crisis. *Newsweek*. Available at **www.newsweek.com/2010/07/10/the-creativity-crisis.html**

- Calkins, L., Ehrenworth, M., & Lehman, C. (2012). *Pathways to the Common Core: Accelerating achievement*. Portsmouth, NH: Heinemann.

- Case, R. (2012, Sept. 22). Personal communication.

- Case, R. (2005, Spring). Moving critical thinking to the main stage. *Education Canada 45*(2), 45-49.

- Conference Board. (2006). *Are they really ready to work? Employers' perspectives on the basic knowledge and applied skills of new entrants to the 21st century workforce*. New York: Author.

- Conley, D. (2007). *Redefining college readiness*. Eugene, OR: Educational Policy Improvement Center.

- Conley, D. (2011). *Redefining college readiness, Volume 5*. Eugene, OR: Epic Policy Improvement Center.

- Edutopia. (2011, Aug. 25). *Resources and downloads for teaching critical thinking*. Available at **http://www.edutopia.org/stw-kipp-critical-thinking-resources-downloads#graph2**

- Expeditionary Learning. (2011). *Evidence of success*. New York, NY: Author.

- Ferlazzo, L., & Sypnieski, K. (2012). *The ESL/ELL teacher's survival guide: Ready-to-use strategies, tools, and activities for teaching English learners of all levels*. San Francisco, CA: Jossey-Bass.

- Finkelstein, N., Hanson, T., Huang, C.-W., Hirschman, B., & Huang, M. (2010). *Effects of problem based economics on high school economics instruction*. (NCEE 2010-4002). Washington, DC: Institute of Education Sciences, U.S. Department of Education.

- Fletcher, A. (2002). *FireStarter Youth Power Curriculum: Participant Guidebook*. Olympia, WA: Freechild Project.

- Hixson, N.K., Ravitz, J., & Whisman, A. (2012). *Extended professional development in project-based learning: Impacts on 21st century teaching and student achievement*. Charleston, WV: West Virginia Department of Education, Division of Teaching and Learning, Office of Research.

- IBM. (2010). *Capitalizing on Complexity: Insights from the Global Chief Executive Officer Study*. Somers, NY: IBM Global Business Services. Available from: **http://public.dhe.ibm.com/common/ssi/ecm/en/gbe03297usen/GBE03297USEN.PDF**

- International Youth Foundation. (2012). *Opportunity for action: Preparing youth for 21st century livelihoods*. Baltimore, MD: Author. Available from **www.microsoft.com/presspass/presskits/citizenship/docs/FinalOpp_for_Action_Paper.pdf**

- Jerald, (2009). *Defining a 21st century education*. Alexandria, VA: Center for Public Education.

- Johnson, D.W., & Johnson, R. T. (2009). An educational psychology success story: Social interdependence theory and cooperative learning (Abstract). *Educational Researcher, 38*(5), 365- 379. Available from **http://edr.sagepub.com/content/38/5/365.abstract**.

- Lenz, B. (2012, Sept. 26). Resources for designing a political campaign ad project. Edutopia [blog]. Available from **http://www.edutopia.org/blog/political-ad-project-pbl-resources-bob-lenz**

- Lindsay, J., & Davis, V. (2012). *Flattening classrooms, engaging minds: Move to global collaboration one step at a time*. Upper Saddle River, NJ: Pearson.

- Marzano, R., & Heflebower, T. (2012). *Teaching and assessing 21st century skills: The classroom strategies series*. Bloomington, IN: Marzano Research Laboratory.

- Markham. T. (2010, Sept. 12). The 21st century dilemma: Can we teach creativity? [Web log post] Available at **http://www.thommarkham.com/blog/default/the-21st-century-dilemma-can-we-teach-creativity/**

- Mergendoller, J. R., Maxwell, N. L., & Bellisimo, Y. (2006). The effectiveness of problem-based instruction: A comparative study of instructional methods and student characteristics. *Interdisciplinary Journal of Problem-based Learning, 1*(2), 49–69.

- Park, A., & Bailey, D. (n.d.) Science lab: Rotten tomatoes. *Think and Wonder* [blog]. **https://sites.google.com/site/farbeyondzebra/science-lab**

- Penuel, W. R., Means, B., & Simkins, M. B. (2000). The multimedia challenge. *Educational Leadership*, 58, 34-38.

- Rindone, N. K. (1996). *Effective Teaming for Success*. Presented at the workshop for the

- Kansas State Department of Education, Students Support Services, Boots Adams Alumni Center, University of Kansas, Lawrence, Kansas.

- Robelen, E. (2012, Feb. 2). States mulling creativity indexes for schools. *Education Week*. Retrieved Jan. 21, 2013, from **http://www.edweek.org/ew/articles/2012/02/02/19creativity_ep.h31.html**

- Schrage, M. (1990). *Shared Minds*. New York, NY: Random House, 140.

- Slavin, R. (1996). Research on cooperative learning: What we know, and what we need to know (PDF). *Contemporary Educational Psychology 21*, 43-69. Available from **http://www.konferenslund.se/pp/TAPPS_Slavin.pdf**.

- Treffinger, D., Young, G., Selby, E., & Shepardson C. (2002). *Assessing creativity: A guide for educators*. Storrs, CT: The National Research Center on the Gifted and Talented, University of Connecticut.

- Vega, V. (2012, Dec. 3). Project-based learning research: Evidence-based components of success. *Edutopia*.org. Available from **http://www.edutopia.org/pbl-research-evidence-based-components**

- Wessling, S., Lillge, D., & VanKooten, C. (2011). *Supporting students in a time of core standards: Grades 9-12*. Urbana, IL: National Council of Teachers of English.

- Woolley, A., & Malone, T. (2011, June). Define your research: What makes a team smarter? More women. *Harvard Business Review*.

Index

A

assessment
    of collaboration, 56-58, (rubric) 127-128
    of communication, 81-82, (presentation
        rubrics) 129-132
    of creativity and innovation, 104-106, (rubric)
        133
    of critical thinking, 34-35, (rubric) 126
    of presentations (rubrics) 129-132

B

Be an Entrepreneur project, 66-69
Berger, Ron, 54
brainstorming, 99, 101

C

Café conversations, 72
Campaign Ad Project, 21-24
Case, Roland, 19, 24-25, 34
Catalina Foothills School District, 119
charette, 103
Classroom Look-fors
    Collaboration, 42
    Communication, 65
    creativity and innovation, 90
    critical thinking, 20
collaboration, 38-61
    assessment, 56-58
    Classroom Look-fors, 42
    in Common Core, 40, 60-61
    in PBL, research on, 44, 141
    definitions of, 12
    rubric for, 127-128
    technology tools for, 58
communication, 62-85
    assessment, 81-82
    Classroom Look-fors, 65
    in Common Core, 64
    in PBL, research on, 68
    definition of, 12
    rubrics for presentations, 129-132
    technology tools for, 83

Common Core State Standards, 9, 13-16, 18,
    36-37, 40, 60-61, 64, 84-85, 88, 108-109, 112
Connect/Extend/Challenge protocol, 33
creativity and innovation, 86-109
    assessment, 104-106
    Classroom Look-fors, 90
    in Common Core, 88, 108-109
    definition of, 12
    in PBL, research on, 93
    rubric for, 133
    technology tools for, 107
critical thinking, 18-37
    assessment, 34-35
    Classroom Look-fors, 20
    in Common Core, 18, 36-37
    in PBL, research on
    definitions of, 11, 19-20, 27
    rubric for, 126
    technology tools for, 35
Critical Thinking Consortium, The, 19 27, 34,
    143
curriculum mapping, 119
Curtis, Paul, 117

D

Driving Question, 5
    for critical thinking, 25-26

E

Edmodo, 4, 58, 59, 113
**English Language Arts Common Core State
    Standards**, 9, 13-16, 18, 36-37, 40, 60-61, 64,
    84-85, 88, 108-109
English Learners in PBL, 78, 79, 80, 81
Envision Schools, 117-119
equity and PBL, research on, 141
Essential Elements of PBL, 5-6
Expeditionary Learning, 8, 54, 114

F

Foundation for Critical Thinking, 27
**Frequently Asked Questions about PBL and
    21st Century Learning**, 138-139